JUBILEE

AMERICA'S SET TIME

RICH McCASLAND

JUBILEE

AMERICA'S SET TIME

Editor Christy Smith
RICH McCASLAND

Whosoever Press books may be ordered through booksellers or by contacting:

Whosoever Press
10749 AL Hwy 168
Boaz, AL. 35957

www.whosoeverpress.com
1-256-706-3315

ISBN: 978-0-615-81746-0
Library of Congress Control Number: Applied For

Printed in the United States of America

Whosoever Press Date: 12/5/2017

You may purchase a beautiful 16" x 20" image of the TIME IS RUNNING OUT front cover at: www.RevivalFires.org

Whosoever Press adamantly supports the nation of Israel.

DEDICATION

This book is dedicated to the memory of my spiritual brother Steven Thomas Soderling. I regard his advice daily. God called him to heaven way too early for those left here.

"Honor all men. Love the brotherhood. Fear God. Honor the King."

1 Peter 2:17

TABLE OF CONTENTS:

FOREWORD

One scripture that seems to be overlooked in Western Christianity today is 1 Thessalonians 5:20, *"Despise not prophecyings."* The definition for despise means "to feel contempt or a deep repugnance for." The word prophecy (ings) means "a discourse emanating from divine inspiration and declaring the purposes of God, whether by reproving and admonishing the wicked, or comforting the afflicted, or revealing things hidden by foretelling future events."

Why would anyone that names the name of Jesus Christ as his or her Lord and Savior, despise divine inspiration? The Bible through the apostles Peter and Paul warns us that in the last days, we would experience perilous times, and people would be walking after their own lusts. They also warn us that some individuals would be willingly ignorant of the coming of Jesus Christ, and would deny the power of God (2 Peter 3:2-7; 2 Timothy 3:1-5). However, the Apostle Paul tells us that those that love Jesus can know the deep things of God. His Spirit reveals the deep things and mysteries of God to us (1 Corinthians 2:9-13).

In the King James Version of the Bible, the word "prophecy" is found 90 times. As you read this book, you will hear the word Gematria mentioned and defined. Interestingly, the 18th letter of the Hebrew alphabet letter *Tsadi* has a Gematria of 90. Tsadi has a picture meaning that is a reference to a righteous person. Why is this so important? The importance can be found in this book.

Personally, I've been teaching and evangelizing the Gospel since 1988. Currently, I'm in my 29th year of a radio ministry. I've taught Sunday school at church since the early 1990's. I've heard thousands of messages preached and/or taught by ministers from different denominations. In 2009, the Lord Jesus began to move me from just expository preaching and teaching to prophetic preaching and teaching. My wife, Tonya, and I have been friends with Richard McCasland since 2011. During the summer of 2016,

Rich shared his "Supernatural Revelation" with me, my wife, and some other close friends. As the 2016 presidential election began to unfold, Tonya and I were in amazement! We continue to be astonished as things unfold.

I would like to emphasize that Richard received this revelation BEFORE and not after the election! In the spring of 2017, Tonya, Rich and I attended a prophetic conference, and one of the speakers preached about Donald Trump and the King Cyrus connection. To our amazement, much of what the speaker shared was in alignment with what our friend Rich had shared with us many months prior. Jesus said in Matthew 18:16, *"But if he will not hear thee, then take with thee one or two more, that in the mouth of two or three witnesses every word may be established."*

I hope that you find *Jubilee America's Set Time* an interesting and revelatory read. If someone is not that into prophecy and end time events, they will be after reading this book. While reading, please keep an open mind. Be sure to reference the scriptures and check how the events coincide with prophecies. For those individuals that still have doubt, I would like to leave this passage for them: Romans 3:4 *"God forbid: yea, let God be true, but every man a liar; as it is written, that thou mightest be justified in thy sayings, and mightest overcome when thou art judged."*

Jarrod E. Shields
Snead State Community College, in Boaz, Alabama
Physics, Physical Science, Physical Geography Instructor
25 years teaching in the science field

Evangelist/Teacher of prophecy
Radio ministry for 29 years on WBSA 1300 AM/93.5 FM Boaz, Alabama

INTRODUCTION

God is infallible and sovereign; He knows every detail of the future. He sees what is yet to happen with as much certainty to what has already happened. Isaiah 46:10 informs us that He announces the end from the beginning. God exists in the realm called eternity; He projects Himself through time to fulfill His own purpose and plan. He is the Alpha and the Omega. God doesn't have any past or future; He has only one tense the present. Time is no hindrance to Him. Prophecy for God is as He says it will be, proclaiming in advance things not yet done. It should come as no surprise that the Word of God contains many predictions of the future. It is one of His many gifts to believers. Biblical prophecy is a wonderfully intricate puzzle that God has given us. I find it very exciting to see how it all fits together.

Educated people, through prejudice, say Bible prophecies are obscure; and, the ignorant of their want of learning. The Bible is a sealed book to every person, learned or unlearned. When a person begins to study it with a simple heart and a teachable spirit, they may, therefore, learn the truth and the will of God. Finding God is to approach him. And if the heart be full of love and fear, out of the abundance of it the mouth will speak (see Isaiah 29:11-14).

We as Christians need to be armed with the truth about the future so that it will change the way we live our lives. Generally speaking, the Christians who have been the most interested in prophecy, who have studied it and understood it clearly, are the most dynamic Christians I have ever known. They are serving God and reaching out to the lost because they have come to grips with the future and understand how the future impacts the present. From the very creation of the world, God set in motion His appointed times, cycles, and seasons. God has plans for the future so that we will live righteously in the present. There is a certain *"set time"* for God's great action.

September 2015, I viewed the last of the lunar eclipses of the *Four Blood Moon Tetrad*. The four blood moons many believed were to

1

be the final heavenly warning from God signaling the *End of Days*. Prophetic

Forecasters, like weathermen, predicted catastrophic storm events in September as the current *Shemitah Sabbath Year* was coming to a close with a *solar eclipse*. Church attendance increased, and many believed Wall Street was going to crash. There were predictions of cash shortages, and a run on banks was expected. Preppers stored up food supplies and other resources as they also expected shortages.

Many Christians in America also discerned these signs and also prepared themselves spiritually for treacherous worldly future events as there had been an incredible amount of buzz about September. In particular, there had been a tremendous amount of speculation about the date of September 23rd. I too came to this conclusion as there was just way too many "coincidences" to ignore.

There were a couple of things about September 23rd we knew for sure. First of all, *Yom Kippur*, the holiest day to the year in Judaism fell on that day. It is the most solemn of all of the holy days in the Bible, and it is commonly connected with repentance and the judgment of God.

Secondly, we knew that Pope Francis would be arriving at the White House to meet with President Barack Obama on September 23rd. Then afterward, he was to visit the city of Philadelphia. Some suggested that the timing of this event was highly unusual. Pope Francis is the 266th Pontiff of the Roman Catholic Church and was meeting with President Obama on the 266th day of the year. The timing of their meeting led many to wonder if "something is being birthed" on that day since 266 days is the typical human gestation period from conception to birth.

But both of those events were not that unusual. Yom Kippur happens every year, and presidents have met with popes in the past. Still, without a doubt, the month of September did appear to be extremely significant.

September 13th – 29th Day of Elul ended the Shemitah Sabbath Year.

September 13th – Partial lunar eclipse.

September 14th – Rosh Hashanah, "The Jewish Feast of Trumpets."

September 15th – The Jade Helm military exercises scheduled to end.

September 15th – The 70th session of the UN General Assembly began.

September 20th - The "World Week for Peace in Palestine Israel."

September 21st – The UN International Day of Peace.

September 23rd – Yom Kippur, "The Jewish Feast Day of Atonement."

September 23rd – Pope Francis arrives at the White House to meet with Barack Obama.

September 24th – The Pope addresses a joint session of the US Congress.

September 26th – Pope Francis arrives in Philadelphia and speaks at the Independence Mall.

September 28th – The first day of "The Jewish Feast of Tabernacles;" the last of the four blood moon lunar eclipses during 2014-15 was a Super Moon and was distinctly observable over the city of Jerusalem.

Alarm bells were sounding loud to many Christians who study the Bible, and the prophetic as September 2015 came to a close. Many people dismissed the blood moon phenomenon, but history has seen similar patterns before, and God often reveals in the natural what is going on in the supernatural. We will explore a few of those patterns in more detail later in this text.

As a Christian interested in Bible prophecy, you probably understand now how significant these events could have potentially been. September was an extremely critical month prophetically. I still do believe all these signs are signaling major future prophetic events in America's future.

Since then, however, the pace has slowed, and scoffers are feeling relieved as they think it was a "false alarm." Many are back to their normal lives scantly attending church, *"conformed to this world"* (see Romans 12:2).

Without a doubt, I still believe that we are currently living in the last days of normal life in America; I think the prophetic forecasters were right to predict a storm to bear witness. I think we did go through the eyewall of a prophetic storm and are currently in the calm center like the *"eye of a hurricane."* We will have to pass through another eyewall of a prophetic storm for spiritual fulfillment before we can rest (Hebrews 4). Buckle up your seatbelts!

How can we prepare? What do we need to do? Hosea 4:6 tells us that our people are destroyed because of the lack of knowledge. More than ever, Christians need to study the Bible more, showing ourselves approved and rightly dividing the word of truth (2 Timothy 2:15). It's entirely possible to have a thorough knowledge of the Bible, yet miss what God is doing in the earth at any given time (Matthew 16:1-3). With the present status of unbelief in America, now is the time to subscribe even more vigorously to the Great Commission.

"And Jesus came and said to them, all authority in heaven and on earth has been given to me. Go ye therefore, and teach all nations, baptizing them in the name of the Father, and of the Son, and of the Holy Spirit: Teaching them to observe all things whatsoever I have commanded you: and, lo, I am with you always, even unto the end of the world."

Matthew 28:18-20

As far back as September 2015, the Holy Spirit gave me a dream on "set time" where I saw a friend, Zachary Drew, Co-Host of the *Jim Bakker Show* and former Host at *Revelation in the News*, teaching on the subject. I shared it with him, as both of us didn't know at the time what it meant. I asked the Holy Spirit to reveal.

Nine-months later, on Sunday morning in June 2016, my local church hosted a Prophetess of God. No one in the Church had known her previously nor had met her until that morning service. She called the pastor two days before and asked him if she could speak. She told the pastor she had a word from God to the church and many of its members.

She preached a wonderful message to the congregation and started to prophecy to the attendees and pastor. Then suddenly she said, "brother in the yellow shirt, can I talk to you?" I looked around and realized it was I wearing the yellow shirt. "Brother Numbers," she said. The Prophetess had no idea I have degrees in both Accounting and Economics. Sister Sharon Fletcher continued to prophecy a message from God over me and about a future project. It elevated my spirit as the message was very detailed as only God could declare. *"For I know the plans I have for you, plans to prosper you and not to harm you, plans to give you hope and a future."*

Jeremiah 29:11

I didn't think God would act so quickly. The very next day on a business trip to Plano, Texas, I was scheduled to see my friend, Pastor Scott Fenton. He had been in Israel recently, and I was looking forward to seeing his pictures and hearing his stories. Driving through the beautiful Amish Countryside of Southeast Oklahoma, I was reminded of last year's events. I prayed out loud in my pick-up truck, as I often do while driving alone. While in prayer regarding what the Prophetess had told me the night before, suddenly with my eyes wide open and continuing down the highway, God downloaded a "Supernatural Revelation" directly into my inner-spirit man, visions, and patterns of future prophetic events for America.

"Call unto me, and I will answer thee, and show thee great and mighty things, which thou knowest not."

Jeremiah 33:3

It felt as though, it was the sensation one experiences when dropping on a roller coaster or while driving on a road with a short incline that has a sharp drop, and it is felt in the belly. I felt intense emotion in my gut similar to the one felt when you hear bad news; you might feel your "heart-drop" or experience a "heartache." It was not a bad feeling; however, for eight hours it was a constant feeling that radiated throughout my body, especially high up in my chest all the way back to Stillwater, Oklahoma. God spoke directly into my heart. God was sending out a signal, and I was at His frequency to receive it.

I didn't tell Pastor Fenton what had just happened on my drive, but he must have sensed something in me as we prayed for a long period together before I left. I have never received a Word from God in that way or felt that way. I asked Him in prayer, "Why me LORD?" I sensed the answer in my heart right away to put pen to paper. I can go on to say that I've never penned anything other than what I've pinned on the farm. I will do my best to convey the deep and intense message of the download by laying out a foundation for understanding these events and prophetic cycles.

Later I will explain my conclusions of what I believe God was showing me about the Jubilee and America's Set Time.

"Surely the Lord God will do nothing, but revealeth His secret unto His servants the prophets."

Amos 3:7

SET TIME

"Thou shalt arise, and have mercy upon Zion: for the time to favor her, yea, the set time, is come."

Psalm 102:13

In the Bible, there are scriptures that deal with time. Some of God's plans happen at scheduled times, while others require a fullness of time (Galatians 4:4). God promised us in Genesis 18:14, *"At the appointed time I will return to thee."* God has a sovereign design behind all events. He is the ruler of the universe. Since the creation of the world, God placed in motion His times, cycles, and seasons, a time for everything. *"To every thing there is a season, and a time to every purpose under the heaven."*

Ecclesiastes 3:1

When God's own time is come, neither Rome, nor the devil, nor governments, can prevent the Kingdom of Jesus Christ from extending its bounds. It is God's work to do it, but He has His own appointed season; and we must, with expectation, wait upon Him. *"That in the dispensation of the fullness of the times He might gather together in one all things in Christ, both which are in heaven and which are on earth in Him."*

Ephesians 1:10

God has a sacred calendar of divine appointments, a *"set time."* He wants us to see it, use it, and give us the wisdom to see His patterns, so we don't miss His warnings or blessings. There is a revelation when we observe the appointed seasons of the calendar of God; we will receive His truths, experience His presence, and serve His purpose. God's calendar is designed for the sake of worship and divine encounters. It is defined by His appointed feasts and His declared sacred seasons that He calls us to observe. Think of God's calendar like an alarm clock that reminds us to remember His great deeds and His glorious promises yet to come.

"And the LORD Spake unto Moses, saying, Speak unto the children of Israel, and say unto them, concerning the feasts of the LORD, which ye shall proclaim to be holy convocations, even these are my feasts. Six days shall work be done: but the seventh day is the Sabbath of rest, a holy convocation: ye shall do no work therein: it is the Sabbath of the LORD in all your dwellings. These are the feasts of the LORD, even holy convocations, which ye shall proclaim in their seasons."

Leviticus 23:1-4

The Feast of the LORD is the term used to express "tent meeting" (*mo'edim*); they are assemblies required to take place at scheduled times. God is really serious about His people observing His appointed times when He says in 2 Chronicles 2:4, *"...on the Sabbaths, and on the new moons, and on the solemn feasts of the LORD our God. This is an ordinance for ever to Israel."*

Why make this an ordinance forever? Are there patterns to be revealed in the firmament of heaven on His appointed days as to His plans (Jeremiah 29:11)? Is it possible to anticipate that God is about to appear for the fulfillment of His promises? Is God using the heavenly bodies as His personal billboard to communicate with us? Is God text messaging us? All good questions I hope will be answered in this text. Let's review what He told us at the beginning of creation. On the Fourth day, God told us why He created the heavenly bodies. In Genesis 1:14-15 we read, *"And God said, Let there be lights in the firmament of the heaven to divide the day from the night; and let them be for signs, and for seasons, and for days, and years: And let them be for lights in the firmament of the heaven to give light upon the earth: and it was so."*

Let me make it clear from the beginning. God isn't giving us astronomical information to enhance our stargazing capability; God is giving us a powerful insight of how the heavenly bodies define His holy seasons and festivals as He reveals His glory to us. According to Biblehub.com, in the original Hebraic text, the Bible

8

does not just say that the sun, moon, and the stars will be for signs. Instead, the original Hebraic text says that the sun, moon, and stars are to mark "religious festivals" or "sacred times."

God scheduled His designated moments at the beginning. They were ordained before the foundation of time to meet His people and bless them. "Set time" or the Hebraic word, *mo'edim* (moh-eh-DEEM) signifies the fixed or appointed days of God. Not just any time, but the "*set time*." In looking up the words "*set time*" in the Hebrew, the Blue Letter Bible describes the meaning as:

-Appointed place, appointed times
-Sacred season, set feast, appointed season
-Appointed meeting
-Appointed sign or signal
-Tent of meeting

Pre-determined or set appointments, the *mo'edim* are typically called "Jewish Holidays" but in the Bible are referred to as God's feast days the sacred signs of God for all of His people. Found in the Book of Leviticus chapter 23, the seven feasts: Passover, Unleavened Bread, First Fruits, Pentecost, Trumpets, Atonement, and Tabernacles. Other considerations are the Shemitah and the Jubilee years of release. Knowledge of these appointed times is critical to an understanding of future events.

"Yea, the stork in the heaven knoweth her appointed times; and the turtle and the crane and the swallow observe the time of their coming; but my people know not the judgment of the LORD."
Jeremiah 8:7

As we study the Bible and history, we find that God measured or allotted certain periods of time for both judgment and blessings. One example important to this text is the story of the Jews being held in *Babylonia Captivity.*

Nineveh the *Assyria* capital had fallen, and it was just Egypt and Babylon who were seeking world supremacy. A brilliant young

King of Babylon, *Nebuchadnezzar*, went out and defeated the Egyptians at *Carchemish* in 605 BC (Jeremiah 46:2). He marched on to Judah, during *Jehoiakim's* reign, and took thousands of Hebrews back to Babylon (including Daniel, who became one of the greatest prophets).

Nebuchadnezzar made two more attacks when he heard of rebellion in Judah. Each time he took captives (including Ezekiel the prophet). Only a remnant of the weakest, poorest, and least threatening Jews remained. Nebuchadnezzar set up a puppet king of David's line to sit on the throne of Judah and made him swear an oath of allegiance (2 Chronicles 36:10-12).

King *Zedekiah* was as faithless as the rest of the evil kings of Judah. He then rebelled and allied with other enemies. When Nebuchadnezzar heard of this rebellion, he came back for the last time in 586 BC to reduce Jerusalem to rubble and send the *First Temple* (Solomon's) up in flames. Zedekiah was forced to witness the slaughter of his sons, then his eyes were put out, and he was carried off to Babylon where he remained a prisoner until his death.

2 Kings 24:13-14, *"And he carried out thence all the treasures of the house of the LORD, and the treasures of the king's house, cut in pieces all the vessels of gold which Solomon king of Israel had made in the temple of the LORD, as the LORD had said. And he carried away all Jerusalem, and all the princes, and all the mighty men of valor, even ten thousand captives, and all the craftsmen and smiths: none remained, save the poorest sort of the people of the land."*

There was an appointed time for the Jewish exile in Babylon, and when the weeks were fulfilled; neither bolts nor bars could longer imprison the remnant of the LORD. Scripture refers to this in

Jeremiah 25:9-12 that Judah would serve Babylon for 70 years, predicting the Jewish captivity.

After the fall of Babylon according to the Book of Ezra, the Persian King, *Cyrus the Great,* ended the exile near 539 BC, the year after he captured Babylon. Cyrus freed the exiled Jews, and they were permitted to return to Judah in the first year of his reign with the "*Decree of Cyrus.*"

What many people do not realize in reading Isaiah 44:28, is that Cyrus was named by the prophet long before the monarchy was even born. Later in Isaiah 45:1, the LORD calls him His "anointed." Isaiah also prophesied the reigns of Uzziah, Jotham, Ahaz, and Hezekiah, (all) kings of Judah (Isaiah 1:1). His ministry occurred possibly between 740 – 701 BC. This was some one hundred and fifty years before Cyrus was born.

The Decree of Cyrus - "*And in the first year of Cyrus, King of Persia, at the completion of the word of the LORD from the mouth of Jeremiah, the LORD aroused the Spirit of Cyrus, King of Persia, and he spread a proclamation throughout his kingdom, and also in writing, saying: So said Cyrus, the King of Persia; All the kingdoms of the earth gave to me, the LORD, God of heaven, and He commanded me to build Him a House in Jerusalem, which is in Judea. Whoever is amongst you of all His people, God be with him, and he should ascend to Jerusalem, which is in Judea. And he should build the House of the LORD; God of Israel He is the God Who is in Jerusalem. And whoever remains from all the places where he resides, they should promote him the people of his residence with silver and with gold and with possessions and with cattle, with the donation to the House of God, which is in Jerusalem*"

Ezra 1:1-4

"*Thou shalt arise, and have mercy upon Zion: for the time to favor her, yea, the set time, is come.*"

Psalm 102:13

The *"set time"* for the exiles did come in the appointed season, and when that period arrived, they were blessed with the re-establishment of the city of Jerusalem and the *Second Temple*.

According to the Bible, when the Jewish exiles returned to Jerusalem following the Decree from Cyrus (2 Chronicles 36:22-23, Ezra 1:1-4), construction started in 537 BC on the *Second Temple* at the original site of Solomon's *First Temple*. After a relatively brief halt due to opposition from peoples who had occupied the city during the Jewish captivity (Ezra 4), work resumed about 521 BC under *Darius the Great* (Ezra 5) and was completed during the sixth year of his reign about 516 BC. It took 21 years to finish rebuilding the Second Temple, and this is equal to three periods of seven (777).

Can coming events cast their shadows? Indicating an event before it takes place? Can the story of the Babylon Captivity be an example of appointed patterns of future events for Israel and America? Has the *"set time"* come? *"That which hath been is now; and that which is to be hath already been; and God requireth that which is past."*

Ecclesiastes 3:15

TIMES AND SEASONS

"He answered and said unto them, when it is evening, ye say, it will be fair weather; for the sky is red. And in the morning, it will be foul weather today; for the sky is red and lowering. O ye hypocrites, ye can discern the face of the sky; but can ye not discern the signs of the times?"

Matthew 16:2-3

Jesus cried out to us to discern the signs of the times. He established truth in His Word, continues to work through the lives of men, and reveals Himself according to times, seasons and cycles. Did you know that, in the Bible, there was a group of people that always knew just what to do? They could discern the times and seasons and had such awareness and discernment that a whole nation followed them and waited for their judgment. They were called the *Sons of Issachar*, and they were one of the twelve tribes of Israel.

"And of the children of Issachar, which were men that had understanding of the times, to know what Israel ought to do; the heads of them were two hundred; and all their brethren were at their commandment."

I Chronicles 12:32

Issachar was the ninth son of Jacob and the fifth son of Leah (Genesis 30:17-18). His children were very influential and wise religious teachers. Issachar's name means either "he will bring a reward" or "man of wages." The tribe would devote their time to the study and teaching of the *Torah,* could understand time, and could discern the seasons. Issachar was one of three of the twelve tribes that moved together. Issachar was positioned strategically with Judah and Zebulun (Numbers 2:5; 10:14-15).

Zebulun, the tenth son of Jacob and the sixth and last of Leah, was the tribe of wealth and trade. The members traditionally were merchants and provided financial support in exchange for a share of Issachar's spiritual reward. *Judah* was the fourth son of Jacob and Leah. His name meant "to be praised." His was the warrior tribe and was the first tribe to move with authority and boldness.

Issachar had special significance; they could give great insight to the schedule of appointed times. The Issachar tribe had several distinct characteristics. According to the *Targum*, they knew how to ascertain the periods of the sun and moon, the intercalation of months, the dates of solemn feasts, and could interpret the signs of the times.

The Targum denoted the oral spoken paraphrases given in the synagogues of the rendering of Bible scriptures which was often spoken in Aramaic. These spoken words were written down to explain in the common language for the listeners to comprehend.

Issachar's descendants studied the movements of the stars and planets and understood chronological time. They were responsible for calling the whole nation together when the stars aligned. They knew God's *"set time."* The Jewish feast days were based upon the lunar calendar, with consideration also given to the movement of the sun. This was significant as Israel had to gather to worship God on specific days on this heavenly calendar.

When signs and wonders happened in the heavens (with the sun, moon, and stars), the Sons of Issachar knew how to interpret the meaning of those events. The Sons of Issachar understood chronological time, but they also understood spiritual and political time. They could discern what God was doing and when He was doing it. They knew when one move of God was ending and another one was beginning. They could discern when a leader was falling, and another leader was rising. They could even tell you who the next leader should be. They were not only full of wisdom, but the Sons of Issachar also excelled in the knowledge of God's law (Torah).

God chose the Sons of Issachar as one of the three tribes to go out in front of Israel whenever the nation moved. Judah (the praising people) went first; then Issachar (the wise and discerning ones) and Zebulun (the financiers). That's quite a combination!

That ability gave them inside knowledge and understanding of God's activities. They were not taken by surprise when things happened. They had influence as a result of their unique ability to understand the times and seasons. They knew what Israel should do and when it should be done. The nation followed their example.

The good news is you, and I can have the same anointing of the Sons of Issachar! We can have the same ability to discern the times and seasons! God wants us to understand the times and seasons so we can prosper and have the wisdom to advance. I pray that the anointing of the Sons of Issachar becomes alive in you now! Amen!

Pay attention new ordained Sons of Issachar; we're about to go somewhere! God has given us signs and instructions of what to watch for and what to do, regarding the return of His son Jesus. I would not presume to suggest when Jesus will return. He made it clear that it is not for us to know the exact time (Matthew 24:36), but clues tell that His return may be near. Fulfillment of prophecy is a clear indication that the last days are upon us. Can you discern the times?

These signs will all come together in a generation. However, if we are to understand the true purpose of the heavenly signs, we must not embrace the perversion of astrology. Many have become obsessed with trying to untangle the mysteries of end-time prophecies through this misapplication.

Instead, we must discover God's original intent at creation and see how God stamped a unique visible picture of His story in the heavens. Watch the signs and weigh them for yourself. Not checking things out in personal Bible study is simply lazy and foolish. Our comprehension should include the ability to perceive times and seasons by recognizing how God's people understood these things in the beginning, like the Sons of Issachar.

The Bible speaks of the utter nonsense of believing the stars in heaven can influence and govern your private life: *"Thou art wearied in the multitude of thy counsels. Let now the astrologers, the stargazers, the monthly prognosticators, stand up, and save thee from these things that shall come upon thee. Behold they shall be a stubble; the fire shall burn them; they shall not deliver themselves from the power of the flame: there shall not be a coal to warm at, nor fire to sit before it."*

Isaiah 47:13-14

Astrology is a belief that the position of the stars at certain times induces the effect of good or bad luck in your daily routine. While astrology and star worship is forbidden in Scripture, there is a study of Biblical astronomy that can reveal clues to Biblical signs in the heavens as they pertain to the last days. These are the signs in the sun, moon and stars that Christ spoke of in Luke 21:25-28.

The sun, moon, and stars were created for more than to simply give light to mankind. Prior to calendars, the sun determined the cycle of the day and year; and, the moon determined the cycle of the month. Early primitive cultures used a solar calendar, but Jewish seasons were determined by a lunar calendar. Most of us have lived our entire lives according to a solar calendar of 365.25 days in a year, not knowing God has a lunar calendar that is quite different from ours. Our clocks and calendars are only accurate because as they are synchronized with the heavens, just as our lives are only accurate when in harmony with God. I'll explain later in this text.

"The heavens declare the glory of God; and the firmament showeth His handiwork."

Psalm 19:1

The stars are the reference for time. In the circuit of the heavens in modern astronomy, the sky (celestial sphere) is divided into 88 regions called *constellations*, generally based on the asterisms of Greek and Roman mythology. Those along the *ecliptic plane* are the constellations of the zodiac. The ancient Sumerians, and later the Greeks (as recorded by *Ptolemy*), established most of the northern constellations in international use today.

The 88 constellations depict 42 animals, 29 inanimate objects, and 17 humans or mythological characters. Jewish rabbinical sources point out that for 2,500 years, men had no written record of the words of God. According to the Jewish Historian Josephus, God gave to the first man, Adam, the secrets of the universe. Adam then passed these heavenly mysteries on to his son Seth and passed them on to their children, including one of the first prophets in the Bible, Enoch.

Numerous times in scripture, the sun, moon, and stars became a visible picture of a future prophetic promise:

* Abraham was told his seed would be as the "stars of heaven."

Genesis 21:7

* Joshua was given the heavenly sign of the sun staying in one spot.

Joshua 10:13

* Hezekiah was given the sign of the sundial going backwards.

Isaiah 38:8

* The Magi saw a star in the east as the sign the Messiah was born.

Matthew 2:2

* Signs in the sun, moon, and stars with nations confused by the roaring of the sea.

Luke 21:25

* A woman clothed with the sun and the moon with a crown of twelve stars.

Revelation 12:1-3

The Book of Job, thought to be the oldest book in the Bible, records a story that goes back to approximately 2150 BC. The stories in the sky of the twelve signs of the zodiac are mentioned as *Mazzaroth* in Job 38:32 - *"Canst thou bring forth Mazzaroth in his season? Or canst thou guide Arcturus with his sons."* Mazzaroth is a Hebrew word which means in general *"The Constellations of the Zodiac."*

Traditions suggest that the names of the stars and the constellations originally had meaning to Adam, Seth, and Enoch, that they were created to serve as a *mnemonic*, a memory tool, to tell a very important story. The constellations in the heavens held a mysterious redemptive story, placed there as a visible reminder of God's appointed plan. It appears that 4,000 years ago, ancient peoples used the same names and meanings of the stars in the heavens. These star pictures, created originally by God, are symbolisms that represent things to come.

Out of 88 constellations, there are 12 major ones that the sun passes through during a solar year. Jacob, the father of modern Israel, had 12 sons who were the heads of the 12 tribes of Israel. These tribes eventually formed the nation of Israel (see Genesis 35:22).

Genesis 49:9 reveals that Judah's tribal emblem is a lion. In the heavens, one of the 12 major constellations is a lion known as Leo. The sun begins its yearly circle in the constellation of the virgin (Virgo) in January, and the year ends in the constellation (Leo), the lion in December. Jesus came the first time, birthed as the Lamb of God from a virgin and will return as the Lion of Judah (Revelation 5:5). God wrote the beginning and the end of our restoration in the heavenly bodies. One can't get away from the Bible even if one doesn't believe it!

ECLIPSES AND BLOOD MOON TETRADS

"And I will show wonders in the heavens and in the earth, blood, and fire, and pillars of smoke. The sun shall be turned into darkness, and the moon into blood, before the great and terrible day of the LORD come."

Joel 2:30-31

Solar eclipses occur when the moon is between the sun, and the earth, with a full eclipse happening when the sun, moon and earth are on almost exactly the same plane. Ancient cultures around the world attributed godly traits to the sun and developed myths around it held ceremonies and even built temples in its honor.

Rabbis in Israel teach that a total solar eclipse is a *"bad omen"* or a warning for the world that darkness is coming because of sin. According to rabbinical interpretations of eclipses, a "solar" eclipse is a sign of trouble for the world, and a "lunar" eclipse is a sign of trouble for the nation of Israel. However, eclipses can be a sign for both Jew and Gentile, as the Apostle Peter the made a precise statement on the Day of Pentecost (Acts 2:17-21) from the Book of Joel about Holy Spirit outpourings and eclipses in the last days.

Eclipses are spectacular to see indeed. No more than seven combined eclipses of the sun and moon can occur in one year. It is very rare to have seven eclipses in one calendar year. The last time was 1982, and the next time will be 2038.

Let's review some interesting facts and history for further investigation. According to Timeanddate.com, three times in the 20th century there were seven total eclipses in one year. During the seven eclipses that occurred in 1917, the Russian Revolution occurred, and World War I was coming to an end. General *Allenby* liberated Jerusalem after 400 years of Turkish rule, and the Balfour Declaration was signed giving the Jews access back to the Holy Land.

During the seven eclipses that occurred in 1973, the *Yom Kippur War* occurred in Israel, and the subsequent *Arab Oil Embargo* economically impacted America and the West. During the seven eclipses in 1982, the *Lebanon War* occurred in Israel and the United States sent the Marines into Beirut. All three times-1917, 1973, and 1982-were filled with implications for both the United States and Israel.

Did you also know that there was a total solar eclipse over Europe on August 21, 1914, only weeks after the outbreak of the World War I? The last time a total solar eclipse crossed the United States from the Pacific to the Atlantic was June 8, 1918. It was visible from Washington State to Florida. *Totality* was observed over Stillwater, Oklahoma, my home! Webster's Dictionary defines Totality as the moment or duration of total obscuration of the sun or moon during an eclipse.

This may not have any relation to the eclipse of 1918, but in the same month of June 1918, the *Spanish Flu Pandemic* spread, infecting 500 million people across the world. That event resulted in the deaths of 50 to 100 million (three to five percent of the world's population) making it one of the deadliest natural disasters in human history.

The first confirmed outbreak in the United States was at Fort Riley, Kansas, then a military training facility preparing American troops for involvement in World War I. Further inquiry discovered that *Haskell County, Kansas* was the original point of origin of the outbreak. Interestingly, totality was observed over that same spot in the same month!

According to NASA, on Monday, August 21, 2017 (*1st of Elul* on the Hebrew Calendar), all 50 States of America will be treated to an eclipse of the sun as it disappears behind the moon, turning daylight into twilight. Twelve states in America will fall under the centerline path of a total solar eclipse. The meaning of 12 is considered a perfect number as it symbolizes God's power and authority. The so-called *"Great American Total Solar Eclipse"* will darken skies all the way from Salem, Oregon to Charleston, South Carolina, along a stretch of land about 70 miles wide. The number 70 embodies God's spiritual order and a period of judgment. Did you know it also takes an estimated 70 hours to read the entire Bible aloud?

On the 233rd day of the year, the first major city under the eclipse is Salem, Oregon. Salem was named after Jerusalem. As the sun casts its shadow over Salem, the sun will be setting in Jerusalem at the exact same time; the sound of shofars blowing in the city will be the start of *Teshuva*. Oregon was the 33rd state added to the Union; the eclipse exits at Charleston, South Carolina, which lies on the *33rd Parallel North*. Jerusalem also lies on the 33rd Parallel North. Jesus is believed to have been 33 when He was crucified in Jerusalem. Charleston is also where the American Civil War started. Could another American Civil War looming?

The coming total solar eclipse is widely called the "Great American Eclipse" because it will be very accessible to so many millions of Americans. A total solar eclipse is a spectacular sight in nature when the sky suddenly darkens, and the sun's shimmering corona becomes visible for two minutes or so. Seeing a total solar eclipse is an intensely emotional experience and a memory to last a lifetime for many.

Twelve and a quarter million Americas live in the path of totality, which is 3.8 percent of the population. The website, Greatamericaneclipse.com estimates another 1.85 to 7.4 million people will visit the path of totality on eclipse day to experience the event. The eclipse will start about 10:16 am in the *Pacific Time Zone*, shadow America midday, and will exit at 2:49 pm in the *Eastern Time Zone.* It will take 1 hour and 33 minutes to cross the country. The longest duration of totality will be 2 minutes and 41.6 seconds in southern Illinois at Makanda. Here are some questions for you to discern. Why will the eclipse only pass through the United States? Could this total solar eclipse be a "bad omen" for the United States? Is there another flu pandemic coming? Could God be giving a direct warning to the United

States (the Great Gentile Nation) to repent or judgment will be coming? Is this the beginning of the "Fullness of the Gentiles" that we read about in Romans 11?

"In those days John the Baptist came preaching in the wilderness of Judea, and saying, Repent ye: for the kingdom of heaven is at hand."

Matthew 3:1-2

The eclipse does occur at the beginning of the "month of repentance," on the *1st of Elul* on the Hebrew Calendar. The eclipse is before the celebration of the Fall Feasts of Trumpets, Atonement, and Tabernacles.

The eclipse appears on the first day of *Teshuva*, the forty-day Jewish season of prayer and repentance (the number forty means a time of testing). At sunset for 40 days, "trump-blasts" from shofars are heard in Jerusalem. It's a time for repentance and intimacy with God leading up to the Day of Atonement. It's a time for the Jews to return (turn back) to the presence of God in prayer and is a warning to avoid judgment. *"The LORD is my light and my salvation."* - Psalm 27:1

The *1st of Elul* is the same time the *Old Testament* tells us that Moses went back up 40 days on *Mount Sinai* to make atonement for the sin of the *golden calf* (Deuteronomy 9:18-25). In the *New Testament*, we find this also begins at the same time Jesus Christ went into the wilderness for 40 days after being baptized in the *Jordan River*.

Furthermore, this is the same time Jonah went to Nineveh in order to tell them to repent before judgment would fall in 40 days (Jonah 3:1-10). Why would the message of a Jewish man have such an impact in Nineveh? Was there a sign in the sky? NASA calculations date the occurrence of the *Bur-Sagale Total Solar Eclipse* on June 15, 763 BC.

Assyrian records also mention this account and record comments such as, "The gods are warning us that we are coming under judgment?" Then, lo and behold! Here comes a wet-smelly dude looking like he spent three days in the belly of a whale and was crying out, *"Yet forty days, and Nineveh shall be overthrown!"* The ancient Assyrians didn't ignore God's Warning. God saw their works, which they had turned from evil, and He didn't destroy Nineveh.

Also in the Old Testament, during the time of the Exodus; the Hebrew spies took 40 days to spy out the *Land of Canaan* (Numbers 13:25). Israel wondered 40 years in the wilderness for their disobedience (Deuteronomy 8:2-5). Goliath taunted King Saul's army for 40 days before a young shepherd boy killed the giant (see 1 Samuel 17:16).

Will the United States have 40 days to repent, or will judgment be dealt? Could war or catastrophic events be looming for the United States? The timing couldn't be more clear for Christian intercessors to pray and humble ourselves before God to heal our land (see 2 Chronicles 7:14).

"Shall not the land tremble for this, and every one mourn that dwelleth therein? And it shall rise up wholly as a flood; and it shall be cast out and drowned, as by the flood of Egypt. And it shall come to pass in that day, saith the LORD GOD, that I will cause the sun to go down at noon, and I will darken the earth in the clear day: And I will turn your feasts into mourning, and all your songs into lamentation; and I will bring up sackcloth upon all loins, and baldness upon every head; and I will make it as the mourning of an only son, and the end thereof as a bitter day."
Amos 8:8-10

"Repent ye therefore, and be converted, that your sins may be blotted out, when the times of refreshing shall come from the presence of the Lord; and He shall send Jesus Christ, which before was preached unto you: Whom the heaven must receive

until the times of restitution of all things, which God hath spoken by the mouth of all His holy prophets since the world began."

Acts 3:19-21

"Whose voice then shook the earth: but now He hath promised, saying, Yet once more I shake not the earth only, but also heaven."

Hebrews 12:26

The following information I share to make you aware. By no means am I predicting an event. I'll report, and you decide.

The eclipse path of August 21, 2017, lies directly over the *"Juan de Fuca Plate"* off the coast of Northern California, Oregon, Washington State, and Vancouver Island in Canada. The Juan de Fuca Plate is capable of earthquakes in magnitude of 9.0 or larger and producing massive tsunamis all the way to Japan.

Yellowstone National Park is located just north of totality. The eclipse path passes just south of the super-volcano-caldera. Experts say the ash cloud from a full-bore eruption would blanket most of the United States with devastating results. If a total solar eclipse can induce geological shifts, then the Yellowstone Caldera will be an excellent site to monitor closely.

The eclipse path on August 21 of totality continues and exits America over the historic *Middleton Place Plantation,* in the *"Summerville Seismic Zone."* In 1886, Charleston, South Carolina, which falls in this zone, experienced the largest quake to ever hit the Eastern United States with a 7.3 magnitude earthquake.

Seven years from now, another total solar eclipse will take place on Monday, April 8, 2024, visible across North America and Central America. Totality will be visible in a narrow strip in North America, beginning at the Pacific coast, crossing northern Mexico into the United States, through the State of Texas (including Dallas, the most populous city along the path of totality also lies on the *33rd Parallel North*), Arkansas, Missouri, Illinois, Kentucky, Indiana, Pennsylvania, New York, and finally the southern parts of the provinces of Ontario, Quebec. It will vanish at the eastern Atlantic Coast of Newfoundland. It will be the 2nd total eclipse visible from the central United States in just 7 years, coming after the August 21, 2017 eclipse.

The path of this eclipse crosses the path of the previous total solar eclipse of August 21, 2017, with the intersection of the two paths being in southern Illinois at Makanda. Remember Makanda? A small land area will thus experience two total solar eclipses within seven years. It just so happens that both of these eclipses go straight through the *"New Madrid Fault Zone."* The town of Makanda sits atop the major center of the fault zone like a hat. Does "X" mark the spot?

The spot forms a picture of the original Hebrew letter *Tav*, the last letter in the Hebrew Alphabet. The letter Tav is like the letter "X" and is formed by crossed sticks or a sign of the cross. In the Hebrew language, it means a mark, signature, identification, and a "covenant sign."

Earthquakes on the New Madrid Fault Zone are not new; they have occurred throughout history and have been among the biggest earthquakes in American history. According to the website new-madrid.mo.us, (the official website for the City of New Madrid, Missouri) earthquakes were felt as far away as New York City, Boston, and Washington D.C. President James Madison and his wife Dolly felt them in the White House. Church bells rang in Boston. From December 16, 1811 through March of 1812, there were over 2,000 earthquakes in the central Midwest, and between 6,000-10,000 earthquakes near the junction of the Ohio and Mississippi Rivers.

In the known history of the world, no other earthquakes have lasted so long or produced so much evidence of damage as the New Madrid earthquakes. Three of the earthquakes are on the list of America's top earthquakes: the first one on December 16, 1811, a magnitude of 8.1 on the Richter scale; the second on January 23, 1812, at 7.8; and the third on February 7, 1812, at 8.8 magnitudes. After the February 7th earthquake (10-times greater than the San Francisco earthquake of 1906), boatmen reported that the Mississippi River actually ran backward for several hours.

However, the earthquakes were preceded by "signs in the heavens" with the appearance of a great comet, which was visible around the globe for seventeen months and was at its brightest during the earthquakes. The comet, with an orbit of 3,065 years, was last seen during the time of the Egyptian Pharaoh, Ramses II, in about 1254 BC. Scholars debate to be near the same time period of the Exodus by the Israelites from Egypt.

Between 1811 and 1812, the comet was called *"Tecumseh's Comet"* and *"Napoleon's Comet"* in Europe. Tecumseh was a Shawnee Indian leader whose name meant "Shooting Star" or "Panther across the Sky"; he was given this name at birth. Tecumseh was traveling throughout the Southeast to build alliances with the tribes. He told the Choctaw, Chickasaw, Muscogee, and many other tribes that the comet signaled his coming.

It was reported that Tecumseh would prove that the "Great Spirit" had sent him by giving them a sign. Shortly after Tecumseh left the Southeast, the "sign" arrived in the form of a major earthquake. During the next year, tensions between colonists and the Native Americans rose quickly. There have been earthquakes that have followed eclipses. On August 11, 1999, a total solar eclipse crested over the country of Turkey, and six days later (August 17, 1999) a 7.4 earthquake killed tens of thousands. What can the Sons of Issachar discern from these signs and wonders? Look up Luke 21:25-28 and read again. I suggest a great spiritual and or physical shaking is coming to our nation. God is going to shake us to wake us, and the majority of Americans are completely unprepared for it. Are you? Is it time to upgrade your earthquake insurance?

Last year I found it very interesting that a string of consecutive "lunar eclipses," four blood moons called a *"Tetrad"* coincided with Israel's holy feast days during both Passover and Tabernacles in 2014-15.

With that, one should mention other tetrads have occurred as well; it's not all that uncommon of an occurrence. According to NASA, one tetrad occurred in 2003-04. Others will be in the future in 2032-33, 2043-44, 2050-51, 2061-62, 2072-73, and 2090-91. The difference between these tetrads is that they do not align with the Jewish holidays as the others do. Only nine times in history since 1 AD has a blood moon tetrad fallen during the first feast and last feasts.

The most recent tetrad dates that did align with Jewish holidays were 1493-94, 1949-50, 1967-68 and 2014-15. Most stunning is that the last three Tetrads have occurred so close in time to each other during the past 65 years The inspired Bible prophets predicted that the moon would become blood (Joel 2:31, Matthew 24:29, Acts 2:20, Revelation 6:12). For centuries, scholars have attempted to ascertain the meaning of this prophecy.

We will begin by taking a look back at history and the tetrads of 1493-94, 1949-50, and 1967-68. These tetrads revolved around significant historical events for America and the nation of Israel. We will together examine and establish patterns how they relate to America and our spiritual Hebraic connection to Israel. Furthermore, with these patterns, they may reveal future prophetic appointed events for America and the nation of Israel with the Four Blood Moon Tetrad of 2014-15. What could the next tetrad bring us?

"The thing that hath been, it is that which shall be; and that which is done is that which shall be done: and there is no new thing under the sun."

Ecclesiastes 1:9

THE FOUR BLOOD MOON TETRAD OF 1493-94

Let's continue with a glance at the history of what happened prior to the Four Blood Moon Tetrad of 1493-94. This was the last tetrad *before* the United States was established and *before* the restoration of the Jewish State of Israel. Remember who sailed the ocean blue in 1492? It was Christopher Columbus sailing for the New World.

Questions I hope to answer with this text: Does America have a Hebraic link with the Jews starting with the discovery of the New World by Christopher Columbus? Was it really the true intension of Columbus to discover a route to Asia? Was the discovery to be a sanctuary for exiled Jews? Did God intend America to be the "Great Gentile Nation" to spread Christianity to the world? I'll report, and you decide.

During the *Spanish Inquisition*, history records the Catholic Monarchy gave the formal verdict for expelling all Jews from Spain. The *Alhambra Decree* (also known as the Edict of Expulsion) was an edict issued on March 31, 1492, by Queen Isabella I of Castile and King Ferdinand II of Aragon. They ordered the expulsion of practicing Jews from the Kingdoms of Castile and Aragon.

Through the decree, it was intended to maintain *Catholic Orthodoxy* in their kingdoms, to eliminate the influence on Spain's large *coversos* population, and ensure they did not revert back to Judaism. Coversos were Jews who had, by choice or necessity, converted to Christianity to survive annihilation. Most were only given three months and ordered to convert to Christianity or leave the country. Under the edict, Jews were promised royal protection for the three-month period before the deadline. They were permitted to take their belongings with them except gold, silver, or minted money. Throughout history, scholars have given widely differing numbers of the Jews expelled from Spain, but is believed to be near 40,000.

28

The punishment for any Jew who did not convert or leave by the deadline was subject to execution. Although records are incomplete, it is estimated about 150,000 persons were charged with crimes by the Inquisition, and about 3,000 were executed as a result. The punishment for a non-Jew who sheltered or hid Jews was the confiscation of all belongings and stripping of hereditary privileges. A majority of Spain's Jewish population had converted to Christianity during the religious persecutions prior to the Decree. It's estimated that half of Spain's remaining Jews converted as a result of the Alhambra decree and persecution in prior years.

Christopher Columbus was believed to have been of both Jewish and Italian Descent, born in Genoa, Italy. His very name *Christopher* means "Christ-bearer." Christopher symbolizes so beautifully the achievement of his namesake. His paternal grandfather is believed to have been a convert who had his name changed from *Colon* to Colombo.

Colon is a Spanish-Jewish name. The name Colombo is synonymous with the name "Jonah," which means "Dove." Jonah was the first Hebrew prophet sent to a Gentile nation by God. His mission was to go to *Nineveh* and cry against it (be a light to them). However, Jonah rose up and fled from *Joppa* on a ship to flee the presence of the LORD; he found himself thrown overboard by his shipmates after they cast lots (Jonah 1:7) during a fierce storm (see the Book of Jonah).

Columbus was raised a Christian, but it appears he was what we would call today a *Messianic-Jew*. Historians continue to debate this, but his use of the Spanish form of his name in his diaries and letters along with certain oddities lend great credence to this fact.

Many followers of Messianic Judaism are ethically Jewish and continue to follow Jewish customs and laws. Most Messianic Jews consider *Jesus* to be the Messiah and as divine as God the Son, in line with mainstream Christianity. This belief is supported by links between Hebrew Bible prophecies and what Messianic Jews (and most mainstream Christians) perceive as the prophecies' fulfillment in the New Testament. Many also consider *Jesus* to be their "chief teacher and rabbi" whose life should be copied. Many English-speaking Messianic Jews refer to Jesus by the Hebrew name *"Yeshua"* or *"Yehoshua"* rather than by the English name *"Jesus."*

Throughout his life, Columbus showed a keen interest in the Bible and biblical prophecies. Columbus often quoted biblical scriptural passages in his letters and logs. Later he cited in his book, <u>*Libro de las profecias*</u> (Book of Prophecies 1505), a compilation of apocalyptical divine religious revelations towards the end of his life, where he considered his achievements not as an explorer, but more of a fulfillment of Bible prophecy.

One medieval notion Columbus believed was that in order for the end of the world or the second coming of Jesus Christ to occur, certain events must first be enacted. One of the events is that Christianity must be spread throughout the world. Another is that a last crusade must take back the Holy Land from the Muslims and that when Christ returns; He will come back to the place He lived and died -Jerusalem.

Carol Delaney, the author of <u>Columbus and the Quest for Jerusalem</u> (2011), argues that Columbus wanted to find gold to finance a new crusade to recapture Jerusalem from the Muslims, believing that Jerusalem must be in Christian hands before Jesus' Second Coming.

In the book, <u>Christopher Columbus and the Matter of Religion</u> (1992), Prof Bryan F. Le Beau, shows the divine inner secession Columbus felt about his voyage as wrote about America in one of his famous letters: "God made me the messenger of the new heaven and the new earth of which he spoke in the Apocalypse of St John after having spoken of it through the mouth of Isaiah, and he showed me the spot where to find it." Scriptural passages cited by Columbus are found in Isaiah 11:11-12.

"And it shall come to pass in that day, that the LORD shall set his hand again the second time to recover the remnant of his people, which shall be left, from Assyria, and from Egypt, and from Pathros, and from Cush, and from Elam, and from Shinar, and from Hamath, and from the islands of the sea. And he shall set up an ensign for the nations, and shall assemble the outcasts of Israel, and gather together the dispersed of Judah from the four corners of the earth."

Ethnic Jews were being persecuted in Spain and throughout Europe. Did Columbus believe his voyage west "of the sea" would later become a refuge for the Hebrew people? Did he believe his new discovery (America) would be the "Great Gentile Nation" to spread Christianity throughout the world? I'm not sure Columbus did, but God set his plans from the beginning to do so.

Nonetheless, history tells us Columbus suggested that sailing west would be a quicker way to reach the *Spice Islands* than the route around Africa. He proposed a plan to reach the Indies by sailing west across the Atlantic.

Columbus had sought an audience from the monarchs *Ferdinand II of Aragon and Isabella I of Castile* to quest financial support for his voyage. The Catholic Monarchs had just completed an expensive war in the *Iberian Peninsula* against the *Nasrid dynasty's Emirate Granada*. It ended with the defeat of Granada and its annexation by Castile, ending all Islamic Rule on the Iberian Peninsula.

The Catholic Monarchs supported Columbus's petition. They were eager to resupply their wealth and obtain a competitive edge over other European countries in the quest for valuable trade with the Indies.

Europeans had long enjoyed a safe land passage, along the *Silk Road*, to the Indies and China, which were sources of valuable trade goods such as spices and silk. With the fall of *Constantinople* to the Ottoman Turks in 1453, the land route to Asia became much more difficult and dangerous. As such, Portuguese navigators tried to find a sea passage to Asia.

Columbus's project, though far-fetched, held the promise of such an advantage. It is believed the voyage could have been funded by confiscated Jewish wealth from the Spanish Inquisition. Columbus, under the auspices of the Catholic Monarchs of Spain, sailed under their flag on his voyage.

On August 2, 1492, thousands of Jewish people departed the intolerance and repression of Spain for Europe, North Africa, and Turkey. One of their ports of departure was *Palos*, the same port from which Columbus had intended to depart. Columbus delayed the voyage one day which is significant, possibly because of his knowledge of Jewish history. The 2nd of August, 1492 fell on the *9th of Av* on the Hebrew Calendar. The one day during the Jewish year that is considered the worst for Jews. According to Jewish tradition, the 9th of Av is considered cursed. This was the anniversary of the destruction of both Jewish Temples in Jerusalem in 586 BC and 70 AD. In the Book of Numbers Chapter 13, it also tells us it's the day ten spies brought an evil report to Moses.

Columbus was at sea for 70 days, and on the morning of October 12, 1492, the 71st day of the voyage, something significant happened; and, instead of arriving at his intended destination, in Asia, Columbus discovered the New World, "America." He landed on an island in the Bahamas Archipelago that Columbus named "San Salvador," which means "Holy Savior."

Here is something to consider. In Bible numerology, the number 70 have represented restoration. Does Columbus's discovery of America appear familiar to the example previously discussed of the Jews being held in Babylonia captivity for 70 years? Then returned to the Holy Land when Cyrus issued the decree to rebuild Jerusalem and the temple? Was this God's *set time*? Could this be the first Hebraic link to America?

In the book, The Life of Christopher Columbus (1838) by Samuel Griswold Goodrich, the author wrote that on the voyage home from the New World, the wind started to blow very furiously, with a swelling sea. The wind continued to increase with violence, and on the succeeding day, the storm grew worse. The waves raged with fury, and Columbus feared all their incredible discoveries would be lost to the world forever. Columbus then ordered lots to be cast (just like in Jonah 1:7), for one of the crew to make a pilgrimage to *The Royal Monastery of Santa María of Guadalupe* in Extremadura, Spain.

All of the crew made the vow to carry the wax covered parchment that Columbus had written out of their full account. A number of beans were selected with one of them marked with a cross. Columbus was the first to put in his hand and drew the bean with the cross. Two more lots were cast, and Columbus had one fall upon him again. The odds of selecting the winning bean 2 out of 3 times are incredible. So much so, that Columbus from this moment, felt religiously bound to the pilgrimage. The wind became less violent, and the next day he saw the Island of Saint Mary (one of the Azores). Eventually, he made it to the safety of the harbor in Lisbon, Portugal.

Over the course of three more voyages to the New World, Columbus visited the Greater and Lesser Antilles, as well as the Caribbean coast of Venezuela and Central America. He claimed all of it for the Crown of Castile. Columbus saw more of his accomplishments in spreading the light of Christianity than the discovery of the New World. He did visit The Royal Monastery of Santa Maria of Guadalupe in Extremadura, Spain after his first voyage where he gave thanks to God for his discovery.

It is believed that Columbus was not the first European explorer to reach the Americas, having been preceded by the Viking expedition led by *Leif Erikson* in the 11th century. However, his voyages helped lead to the future establishment of Catholic Missions in the New World and introduced Christianity to its native peoples.

European contact with the Americas inaugurated a period of European exploration, conquest, and colonization that lasted for several centuries. These voyages had, therefore, an enormous impact on the historical development of the modern Western World.

No nation has supported the Jews more than America, and America has indeed become a sanctuary for the Hebrew people and a protector of Israel. God appointed America to be the light between the oceans, the "Great Gentile Nation" to spread the gospel around the world and *"proclaim liberty throughout all the land."*

TWO NATIONS SPIRITUALLY CONNECTED BY GOD

The United States, like Israel, is a nation dedicated to God. The United States and Israel are the only two nations who at their beginnings, were and are dedicated to God. Blessings promised to Israel through Abraham are the same blessings we have in America. Both nations were founded and built upon a covenant with God (Deuteronomy 28:1-6). This is very important to know and understand because a nation dedicated to God is held to a higher responsibility as opposed to nations that are not.

Our God is master of order and wisdom. In His covenant plan, He promised Abraham land, children, and prosperity. He determined the boundaries of that land and eventually changed the name of Abraham's grandson, Jacob, to Israel, the name of the land. Jacob had sons who became twelve tribes that were each a part of the whole land of Israel. Each tribe of Israel had a *redemptive blessing*. If we bless Israel, we also will continue to be blessed with the same covenant blessings promised to Abraham.

Late in December 1606, English entrepreneurs set sail with a charter from the *London Company* for the New Word to establish a permanent colony. The fleet consisted of three ships, *Susan-Constant, Discovery, and Godspeed,* along with 144 men and boys. In May 1607, this expedition sailed up the Chesapeake Bay region and continued up the James River. On May 14, 1607, they landed on the spot they would later call *Jamestown*. The first permanent English colony in America was founded on the same day that the State of Israel would be founded 341 years later on May 14, 1948. Is this purely a coincidence or is our nation divinely ordained and spiritually connected to Israel?

Most Americans do not know that our nation was dedicated to God by a king. This took place in 1606 when King James of England stated in the *Jamestown Charter* to the major investors in the Virginia Company that the spread the Gospel of the Almighty God will be first and foremost.

35

"We, greatly commending, and graciously accepting of, these desires to the furtherance of so noble a work, which may, by the providence of Almighty God, hereafter tend to the glory of His Divine Majesty, to such people as yet live in darkness and miserable ignorance of the true knowledge and worship of God, and may in time bring the infidels and savages, living in those parts, to humane civility and to a settled and quiet government."

Spreading the gospel was the first goal of the Jamestown settlers. The second part of the 1606 charter is devoted to the rights of the investors to discover and profit. So not only in our conception via the Jamestown settlers, but also when our nation officially stood on its own as a new nation, we were dedicated to God by our first President, George Washington.

America almost didn't have a president. Most of us know our nation's history; we almost failed to win our independence during the Revolutionary War. But did you know America had a Hebrew connection during the war? God delivered a Jewish man to America to help the cause to proclaim liberty throughout the land.

Philadelphia broker *Haym Salomon* (1740-1785) played a vital role in ensuring that the American colonies' fight to win independence from the British crown continued. During the war, he brokered some large financial transactions that kept American soldiers clothed, fed, and armed.

Haym Salomon was a Polish-born American Jewish businessman and political, financial broker during the American Revolution. He helped convert French loans into ready cash by selling *Bills of Exchange*. What is a bill of exchange? According to Investopedia, a bill of exchange is a non-interest-bearing written order used primarily in international trade that binds one party to pay a fixed sum of money to another party at a predetermined future date.

Bills of exchange are similar to checks and promissory notes. They can be drawn by individuals or banks and are generally transferable by endorsements. The difference between a promissory note and a bill of exchange is that this product is transferable and can bind one party to pay a third party that was not involved in its creation. If these bills are issued by a bank, they can be referred to as bank drafts. If they are issued by individuals, they can be referred to as trade drafts. In this way, Haym Salomon aided the Continental Army and was possibly the prime financier of the American side during the American Revolutionary War against Great Britain.

His family descended from Spanish and Portuguese Jews who fled to the Jewish communities of Poland as a result of the Spanish Inquisition of 1492. In 1775, he immigrated to New York City, where he established himself as a financial broker for merchants engaged in overseas trade. Sympathizing with the Patriot cause, Salomon joined the New York branch of the *Sons of Liberty*. From the period of 1781-84, records show Salomon's fundraising and personal lending helped provide over $650,000 (approximately $16,000,000 in today's dollars) in financing to George Washington in his war effort. His most meaningful financial contribution, however, came immediately before the final Revolutionary War battle at *Yorktown*.

In August 1781, the Continental Army had trapped Britain's General *Cornwallis* off the Virginian coastal town of Yorktown. But Washington's war chest was empty, as was that of Congress. Without food, uniforms, and supplies, Washington's troops were close to mutiny. Washington determined that he needed at least $20,000 to finance the campaign. When he was told there were no funds and no credit available, Washington gave a simple but eloquent order: "Send for Haym Salomon." Salomon raised $20,000, through the sale of bills of exchange. With that, Washington conducted the Yorktown campaign, which proved to be the decisive battle of the Revolution, resulting in the birth of America as "One" Nation Under God.

The history of ancient Israel also shows that it was not until the temple of God was built that Israel truly became a nation. It was under the reign of *King Solomon* who built God's Temple where he prayed at the dedication. Solomon was later shown by God in his spirit, there is prosperity on a nation that follows His statutes, but the nation was also given a warning if they turned away from God. A nation ordained by God has a huge amount of responsibility. We see by the Word, that actions will indeed reflect upon a nation.

We read in 2 Chronicles 7:11-22, *"Thus Solomon finished the house of the LORD, and the king's house: and all that came into Solomon's heart to make in the house of the LORD, and in his own house, he prosperously effected. And the LORD appeared to Solomon by night, and said unto him, I have heard thy prayer, and have chosen this place to myself for a house of sacrifice. If I shut up heaven that there be no rain, or if I command the locusts to devour the land, or if I send pestilence among my people; If my people, which are called by my name, shall humble themselves, and pray, and seek my face, and turn from their wicked ways; then will I hear from heaven, and will forgive their sin, and will heal their land. Now mine eyes shall be open, and mine ears attent unto the prayer that is made in this place. For now have I chosen and sanctified this house, that my name may be there for ever: and mine eyes and mine heart shall be there perpetually. And as for thee, if thou wilt walk before me, as David thy father walked, and do according to all that I have commanded thee, and shalt observe my statutes and my judgments; Then will I establish the throne of thy kingdom, according as I have covenanted with David thy father, saying, there shall not fail thee a man to be ruler in Israel. But if ye turn away, and forsake my statutes and my commandments, which I have set before you, and shall go and serve other gods, and worship them; Then will I pluck them up by the roots out of my land which I have given them; and this house, which I have sanctified for my name, will I cast out of my sight, and will make it to be a proverb and a byword among all nations. And this house, which is high, shall be an astonishment to everyone that passeth by it; so that he shall say, Why hath the LORD done thus unto this land, and unto this house? And it shall be answered, because they forsook the LORD God of their fathers, which brought them forth out of the land of Egypt, and laid hold on other gods, and worshipped them, and served them: therefore hath he brought all this evil upon them."*

The birthplace of Israel was upon the Temple Mount in Jerusalem. Most people do not know where the birthplace of our nation took place. It was not in Washington DC, nor was it Philadelphia in 1776. Our nation was indeed conceived in Philadelphia, but we did not become an official nation until April 30, 1789.

This was the day that George Washington was sworn in as America's first president. In fact, there is a very famous statue marking the very spot where he was sworn in. He was inaugurated on the Island of Manhattan, New York City, in front of the *Federal Hall* located on *Wall Street*.

Wall Street is where our country actually became a nation. Federal Hall was at that time home to the first Congress, Supreme Court, and Executive Branch offices. The building is still there, and there is a statue of George Washington standing with his hand stretched out taking the oath of office. Why was his hand stretched out? His statue was portrayed that way so that people could see and remember that George Washington took the oath of office while resting his hand on God's Word, the Holy Bible.

On that day in 1789, things were planned out and seemed to be going smoothly, but as the parade was nearing Federal Hall carrying Washington in a horse-drawn carriage, it was suddenly realized that a Bible had been needed for administering the oath. It was written into the law and, a Bible was required to be part of the ceremony. History shows it was Parade Marshal *Jacob Morton* who hurried off and soon returned with a large 1767 King James Bible, and it was that Bible with which Washington swore his oath of office. The same King James whose charter ordained this country to share the gospel also gave the English speaking people the only authorized Bible in history, the King James Authorized Version of the Bible.

So, on April 30, 1789, our first president was sworn in at Federal Hall, our first seat of government located on Wall Street, Manhattan, New York. After being sworn in, George Washington delivered this nation's first "Inaugural Address" to a joint session of Congress. As the newly inaugurated President, George Washington's first act as President was to lead on foot down the street, the Vice President and members of the Senate and House of Representatives to *Saint Paul's Chapel* for prayer.

Most people do not know that from the beginning, prayer opened up the joint session. It was at Saint Paul's Chapel that our nation was dedicated to God. Our newly founded government joined our president, along with the rest of the nation, upon bent knee and in solemn prayer asked for God's favour and blessing upon this nation.

Our nation and its people were committed to a covenant, by our leader, to God at Saint Paul's Chapel. It was at that very moment that the ground, with which our nation was dedicated, became "hallowed ground." This ground became a special landmark to our nation and to God, like the Temple Mount where Solomon dedicated Israel and her people to God. The very same blessings that parallel Israel are the same blessings for America when we respect God's Word and covenant. However, if America rejects the same ancestral covenant, then our nation will experience disfavour and selective judgments like ancient Israel will occur.

Saint Paul's Chapel is still standing, and the land upon which it sits is a parallel to Israel's Temple Mount. The ground is hallowed to our nation, and many people don't realize or recognize it as such. But all know this place more by its later infamous name, better known as "*ground zero*" after America's 9/11 attack on the "Twin Towers." Borrowing a line from Tulsa, Oklahoma's own famous radio broadcaster, *Paul Harvey*, "and now you know the rest of the story."

Early in 2012, I saw an interview with *Rabbi Jonathan Cahn* on the *Jim Bakker Show* discussing his newly released book. This book titled <u>The Harbinger</u> was a fictional Christian novel about America's 9/11 attack. Having already been fully engaged in studying Bible prophecy, his interview sent me to another level of deep interest in the prophetic. The book showed a parallel to ancient Israel's defiance to God and America's similar defiance. It showed me that our two nations are spiritually connected.

A couple of weeks later I read the entire book. In another Jim Bakker Show, it was announced that Rabbi Jonathan Cahn would again return as a guest in Branson, Missouri. I made the five-hour drive from Oklahoma and joined the lightly attended television audience for the recording of the show. I was able to visit Rabbi Cahn after the taping and asked him questions about the upcoming four blood moons appearing in 2014-15, having just finished *Mark Biltz's* book of the same title. This was before Pastor *John Hagee's* popular book and movie were released about the Tetrad that gave us more prophetic insight to the event. The Rabbi was a gentleman and gracious to answer my questions. Since then I've had the pleasure to meet him again and hear him speak many times at prophetic conferences.

I've been to New York City since I took an interest in <u>The Harbinger</u>, have toured Saint Paul's Chapel, and have walked its sacred grounds in prayer. George Washington dedicated the United States of America to God on April 30, 1789, at his inauguration. He dedicated this land twice; first during his inaugural address at Federal Hall and second in prayer, at Saint Paul's Chapel located on the corner of a place now known as "ground zero." Washington stated in the address at Federal Hall that the nation would prosper and be protected as long as it remained committed to the will and purposes of God.

King Solomon dedicated the First Jewish Temple in Jerusalem to God. When the Israelite people consistently departed from His decrees and laws, judgment came from the LORD. God's first warning was to allow the national hedge of security to be broken and then if the people do not repent, gradually impose more severe consequences.

It was Rabbi Cahn's book that first made me believe there is, in fact, a plausible American spiritual connection to Israel. It gave me the hunger to dig deeper into studying the Bible and prayer. This placed me firmly on a path in my spirit to pray more intensely for America's return to God. I'm convinced God's not done with America, and it is time for new beginnings. The King has one more move!

Below is a summary of the book:

The Harbinger is a 2012 best-selling Christian novel by Rabbi Jonathan Cahn, a Messianic Jew. It suggests that the 9/11 terrorism attack was a divine warning to the United States. Rabbi Cahn ties the 9/11 attacks to a section of Isaiah 9, which describes God vowing to destroy ancient Israel for persistent disobedience towards Him and ignoring the warnings He had sent them. One such warning was a military attack on Israel which caused physical damage to the land; Verses 9 and 10 records that instead of recognizing God's warning and repenting of its sins, Israel defiantly vowed to rebuild using stronger materials and planting stronger trees.

"The LORD sent a word into Jacob, and it hath lighted upon Israel. And all the people shall know, even Ephraim and the inhabitant of Samaria, that say in the pride and stoutness of heart, The bricks are fallen down, but we will build with hewn stones: the sycamores are cut down, but we will change them into cedars. Therefore the LORD shall set up the adversaries of Rezin against him, and join his enemies together; The Syrians before, and the Philistines behind; and they shall devour Israel with open mouth. For all this, his anger is not turned away, but his hand is stretched out still."

Isaiah 9:8-12

Rabbi Cahn says that The Harbinger is a fictional story which nevertheless relates to a real-life connection: a prophecy about ancient Israel that was eventually fulfilled in the eighth century BC when Israel was destroyed, as well as certain events and facts related to the 9/11 terror attacks against the United States in 2001. He calls these events and facts "harbingers," and pleads a case to demonstrate a connection between ancient Israel's destruction and a possible coming destruction of the present-day United States. He also says that ancient Israel received a warning before being destroyed and that the 9/11 harbingers form comparable warnings from God to America.

"Before God judges a nation, He sends warning," Rabbi Cahn has said. "But America, like Israel, has not responded with repentance, but with defiance."

Rabbi Cahn draws parallels between the Kingdom of Israel and modern-day America. He argues that America was founded similar to ancient Israel, and the Founding Fathers envisioned a country based on the rules of God and a Light unto the Nations. He lists a series of warnings or harbingers that were given to ancient Israel before its final destruction by the Assyrians and makes a parallel between each and the events of 9/11.

In his book, Rabbi Cahn lists in <u>The Harbinger</u>, a summary of things he feels we MUST recognize and address individually and as a nation. See the following summary of the nine harbingers.

The Breach: The author argues that the United States just like ancient Israel has breached the covenant it made with God at the time of its foundation. Thus the hedge of God's protection around America was lifted on 9/11 parallel to the way the hedge of protection around ancient Israel was lifted.

The Terrorist: The author argues that similar to the way that the kingdom of Israel was attacked by Assyrians, The United States was attacked by Al-Qaeda. The Assyrians were a Semitic people, children of the Middle East. So too were the terrorists of 9/11.

43

Fallen Bricks: The most visible signs of the attack on ancient Israel were that of the fallen buildings and the ruin heaps of fallen bricks. In 9/11 the most visible site of the attack was also the fallen bricks of the fallen buildings.

The Tower: The harbinger symbolizes the fact that after the Assyrian attack, the kingdom of Israel did not repent from its sins but vowed to rebuild its buildings with its own power. Similarly, the author argues that United States also did not repent from its sins after the warning and continued its path, vowing to rebuild on Ground Zero with its own power.

Gazit Stone: The Israelites carve out quarried stone from mountain rock and took it back to the ground of destruction where clay bricks once stood. Three years after 9/11, a 20-ton quarried rock meant to serve as the cornerstone of the new building was brought to Ground Zero. A ceremony took place over the rock, called the "Freedom Stone," in which New York Governor George Pataki pronounced; "Today, we, the heirs of that revolutionary spirit of defiance, lay this cornerstone and unmistakably signal to the world the unwavering strength of this nation, and our resolve to fight for freedom." Eventually, the stone was permanently removed from Ground Zero after security concerns prompted some redesigning at the site. It now sits in the yard of a stone manufacturing plant on Long Island.

Sycamore: In Isaiah 9:10, the nation of Israel declares that its sycamore trees have been destroyed by the Assyrians during the attack, but they would replace them with cedar trees. After the collapse of the buildings during the 9/11 attacks, a shock wave was created that damaged most buildings around the area. Only one building was not harmed which was Saint Paul's Chapel; it was protected by a sycamore tree that is believed to have absorbed the blast. Rabbi Cahn pointed out that Saint Paul's Chapel was also the place that the government of the United States prayed on the day of the first inauguration of George Washington on April 30, 1789. The sycamore is known today as the 9/11 Sycamore, and a memorial was built for it.

Erez Tree: In Isaiah 9:10, the nation of Israel vows to replace the damaged sycamores with cedars, which are stronger. Two years after the events of 9/11, on November 29, 2003, an actual tree was planted in the place of the original sycamore in front of Saint Paul's Chapel. This tree was a 21-foot spruce tree and was called the Tree of Hope. The tree itself no longer exists. It died, was dug up, destroyed, and not replaced.

The Utterance: Or referred to as "the vow" of defiance. For there to be a parallel with ancient Israel with this harbinger, Rabbi Cahn says a national leader would have to speak the defiant vow to rebuild in the nation's capital. He explains that United States Senator John Edwards did during a 9/11 memorial on September 11, 2004, when he quoted Isaiah 9:10.

The Prophecy: Another parallel with ancient Israel, according to Rabbi Cahn, is that a national leader must utter the Isaiah 9:10 vow as a prophecy, before such events as the replacing of the tree and the bringing of the cornerstone rock to Ground Zero. Rabbi Cahn says this occurred one day after the events of 9/11 when America issued its official response to the terrorist attacks. Senator Tom Daschle, who was the Senate Majority Leader at the time and in charge of the official response, spoke before the Congress. At the end of his speech, he quoted Isaiah 9:10.

The Shemitah: Rabbi Cahn also argues that the financial collapses of the Dow Jones Industrial Average on September 17, 2001, and September 29, 2008 (List of largest daily changes in the Dow Jones Industrial Average: Largest point changes) were also prophetic warnings. He says that both happened on the same date of the Hebrew calendar, the *29th of Elul*, and relates them to the Shemitah, a Sabbath year observed every seven years in Judaism, in which the land isn't cultivated, and debts are canceled. Rabbi Cahn suggests that a third strike might be the collapse of the American power which lies in the nation's economy.

THE FOUR BLOOD MOON TETRAD OF 1949-50

I will continue to build on the case that Israel and America are spiritually connected to each other. Let's examine what happened before the Four Blood Moon Tetrad of 1949-50, the *"first tetrad"* *after* the establishment of the United States and *after* the prophetic fulfillment and restoration of the State of Israel.

President Franklin D. Roosevelt appeared to be sympathetic to the Jewish cause after World War II; his assurances to the Arabs that the United States would not intervene without consulting both parties caused public uncertainty about his position. When Harry S. Truman took office after the death of President Roosevelt in 1945, he became the 33rd President of The United States (33 means promise). He made it very clear that his sympathies were with the Jews and accepted the *Balfour Declaration*.

The Balfour Declaration was a 67-word letter dated November 2, 1917, from the United Kingdom's Foreign Secretary, Arthur James Balfour to Walter Rothschild, 2nd Baron Rothschild, and leader of the British Jewish community. It read as follows:

"His Majesty's government view with favour the establishment in Palestine of a national home for the Jewish people, and will use their best endeavours to facilitate the achievement of this object, it being clearly understood that nothing shall be done which may prejudice the civil and religious rights of existing non-Jewish communities in Palestine, or the rights and political status enjoyed by Jews in any other country."

President Truman initiated several studies of the Palestine situation that supported his belief that, as a result of the *Holocaust*, Jews were oppressed and also in need of a homeland. Throughout the Roosevelt and Truman administrations, the Departments of War and State, recognizing the possibility of a Soviet-Arab connection and the potential Arab restriction on oil supplies to this country, advised against United States intervention on behalf of the Jews. President Truman instructed the State Department to support the United Nations Plan. On November 29, 1947, the plan adopted as "Resolution 181" the United Nations Partition Plan for Palestine, was passed by the General Assembly.

At midnight on May 14, 1948, Israeli Declaration of Independence was proclaimed by *David Ben-Gurion*, the Executive Head of the World Zionist Organization and the chairman of the Jewish Agency for Palestine. Israel was born at once as a nation in one day. This fulfilled Bible prophecy as the prophet foretold in Isaiah 66:8. The proclamation established the first Jewish State in 2,000 years. It declared the establishment of a Jewish State to be known as Israel, which would come into effect on termination of the *British Mandate*.

On the same day, the United States, under President Truman, became the first country to extend any form of recognition, followed by Iran. This happened within hours of the Jewish People's Council gathering at the Tel Aviv Museum and David Ben-Gurion declaring "the establishment of a Jewish State in Eretz Israel, to be known as the State of Israel."

Against his advisors, President Truman stood fast and recognized the provisional Jewish government and authority of the Jewish State. The White House issued the following statement; "This Government has been informed that a Jewish State has been proclaimed in Palestine, and recognition has been requested by the provisional government thereof. The United States recognizes the provisional government as the de facto authority of the State of Israel." It's been said that the United States delegates to the United Nations and top-ranking State Department officials were angered that President Truman released his recognition statement to the press without notifying them first.

Truman indeed was an unusual choice to be used by God. The folksy "Give 'em hell Harry" was beloved by some and hated by others for his colorful language he attributed to his youthful days working on the Santa Fe Railroad. However, the Bible is full of unlikely people that God uses for His purpose.

"I never did give them hell," he once reminisced, "I just told the truth, and they thought it was hell."

Some historians portray President Truman as a dependable supporter of the Jewish State. Others describe him as having been a Pro-Zionist or a Christian Zionist along the lines of Britain's Arthur Balfour or David Lloyd George, who in 1917 got the British government to champion a Jewish Homeland.

Other significant events for Israel during the 1949-50 Tetrad where the first national election in January 1949 and in May 1950, 113,000 Iraqi Jews relocated to Israel and in September, 47,000 Yemeni Jews relocated. Isaiah 11:10-12, Jeremiah 30:3-4, Ezekiel 37 and Ezekiel 38:8 all speak of Jews returning to Israel.

In November 1953, after he had left the presidency, Harry S. Truman traveled to New York to be feted at the Jewish Theological Seminary. When an old friend, Paul Charles Merkley of Christianity Today introduced him as "the man who helped create the State of Israel," Truman responded, "What do you mean 'helped to create?' I am Cyrus!" Truman was referring to the Persian King who overthrew the Babylonians in 539 BC and helped the Jews, who had been held captive in Babylon, return to Jerusalem and rebuild their *Second Temple*.

Truman biographer Michael T. Benson says that Truman's support for Israel was an "outgrowth of the president's religious upbringing and his familiarity with the Bible." But Truman's love for the Bible may have been partly based on his flawed eyesight. The family Bible, with its extra-large print, was one of the few books at home the young Truman could read. Truman cast himself as a consistent proponent of the Jewish State and his love for the Bible.

In the bio Truman, David McCullough writes that when Truman recognized the new State of Israel in May 1948, he had "no regrets" about what "he achieved." Truman's reputed devotion to Israel has become the standard by which subsequent presidents' commitment is measured. In 1982, Richard Nixon described Ronald Reagan as the "most pro-Israel president since Truman."

I believe the biographer failed to explain Truman's true love for Israel. It was more than Truman's religious upbringing and his love of the Bible. It was deeper than that. The root of his love and understanding of the Jewish people started with his family.

When Truman was six, he attended Presbyterian Church School and did not attend a traditional school until he was eight. While living in Independence, Missouri as a young man, he served as the "Shabbos goy" for his Jewish neighbors; doing tasks for them on *Shabbat,* which they were prevented from doing because of rules against work on the Sabbath.

"I call heaven and earth to record this day against you, that I have set before your life and death, blessing and cursing; therefore, choose life, that both thou and thy seed may live."
Deuteronomy 30:19

Focus on the proclamation of the Word of God above; Moses encouraged the people to choose life, and reminded them, (Deuteronomy 30:15-20) this choice not only affects your life, but also the descendants that follow you, "Thy Seed." The blessing of God produces good, beneficial results and enables us to succeed.

I believe there were generational blessings in Truman's family tree, like the kind written in the Book of Deuteronomy. Let's examine Truman's Christian mother, Martha Ellen Young. She was born to Solomon Young, a successful farmer who also had a business running *Conestoga* wagon trains along the *Overland Trail.* It is said, members of the family were southern sympathizers in the Civil War, and several relatives served in the Confederate Army.

Later in life, Martha told of how a band of Union-supporting Jayhawkers destroyed her family's farm one day in 1861, then again in 1863. This harsh treatment left Martha with a lifelong resentment for the Union (Yankees) in the war. She was well known for her Confederate sympathies. A story made the rounds that when she first visited the White House in 1945; she refused to sleep in the Lincoln Bedroom.

Martha attended the Baptist Female College in Lexington, Missouri. She married John Anderson Truman in Grandview, Missouri. Their first son died just a few days after birth. Their second child, another son, was Harry S. Truman, born on May 8, 1884. It was believed, that the child's middle name was the subject of some disagreement between the parents. John Truman wanted it to be Shipp, after his father Anderson Shipp Truman, while Martha wanted it to be Solomon, after her father. In the end, they decided to use only the middle initial 'S' and honor both grandfathers.

Truman's Christian mother blessed him with his middle name "Solomon," named after his maternal grandfather. In the Bible, Solomon was famous for his wisdom; he was the biblical king and a son of David. God personally answered his prayer for wisdom, promising him great wisdom as he did not ask for self-serving rewards like long life or the death of his enemies. The Hebrew Bible credits him as the builder of the *First Temple* in Jerusalem (see 2 Chronicles 7:11-22).

Like King Solomon, President Truman exhibited great wisdom for his love of the Jewish people when he helped with the establishment of the State of Israel during his presidency.

FIRST SPIRITUAL OUTPOURING:
THE GREAT AWAKENING & HEALING REVIVALS

"And ye shall know that I am in the midst of Israel and that I am the LORD your God, and none else: and my people shall never be ashamed. And it shall come to pass afterward, that I will pour out my spirit upon all flesh; and your sons and your daughters shall prophecy, your old men shall dream dreams, your young men shall see visions."

Joel 2:27-28

Let's revisit and reassess history of the spiritual revivals which broke out across America at the time of the Four Blood Moon Tetrad of 1949-50. I will suggest the "outpouring' of the Holy Spirit that began shortly after the prophetic biblical fulfillment and restoration of Israel (Isaiah 66:8) in America was more than just a selective outpouring. I suggest it was greater than what was previously outpoured at a revival in the little *Shearer Schoolhouse* in 1896 near Murphy, in Cherokee County, North Carolina, the place where seven major denominations trace their beginnings.

I suggest it was greater than when the "fire baptism" fell in Topeka, Kansas at the *Bethel Bible School* in 1901. Fire baptism seeded the *Azusa Street Revival*, of California in 1906 and changed the face of Christianity in America. I suggest history will show these revivals which began in the summer of 1948 where, in fact, God's ***"First Major Wave of Rain"*** of the outpouring of the Holy Spirit in America that eventually flooded the entire country with a *Pentecostal Movement.*

What is a Pentecostal Movement? The Pentecostal Movement, initially and known as the Revivalist Movement defined by Wikipedia is a renewal movement within Protestant Christianity that places special emphasis on a direct personal experience of God through the *Baptism of the Holy Spirit*. The term *Pentecostal* is derived from Pentecost, the Greek name for the "Jewish Feast of Weeks." The Feast of Weeks marks the all-important wheat harvest in the Land of Israel (Exodus 34:22), and it

51

commemorates the anniversary of the day God gave the *Torah* to the entire nation of Israel assembled at *Mount Sinai.*

For Christians, this event commemorates the descent of the Holy Spirit upon the 120 followers of Jesus Christ in the *Upper Room,* in Jerusalem traditionally held to be the site of the *Last Supper* as described in the second chapter of the Book of Acts. The inaugural revival occurred on the *Day of Pentecost.*

There's something powerful about a group of people, *"all in one accord, all in one place,"* praying. Can you imagine being there when the heavenly fire fell? Without a doubt, the greatest catalyst for revival is the infusion of the Holy Spirit. In Acts 2:1-4, we read at Pentecost of the tremendous initial outpouring of the Holy Spirit upon the followers of Jesus when, *"suddenly there came a sound from heaven as of a mighty rushing wind (Ruach) ...and they were all filled with the Holy Spirit, and began to speak with other tongues."*

Soon afterward we read of the gathering of believers in Jerusalem when they gladly received the Word of Jesus Christ and were baptized in the *Pool of Siloam* the same day numbering 3,000 souls (Acts 2:41). When they had received the gift of the Holy Spirit, the revival spread from 1 to 12, to 120, to 3,000 and beyond. That's the pattern of Pentecost among God's people to involve ourselves and others into mobilization.

Like other forms of Evangelical believers, Pentecostals adhere to *Bible inerrancy.* The doctrine that says the Protestant Bible is without error or fault in all its teaching of scripture. Pentecostals are distinguished by belief in the *Baptism of the Holy Spirit* that enables a Christian to live a Spirit-filled and empowered life. This empowerment may include the use of spiritual gifts such as speaking in tongues and Divine-Healing.

Jesus said to His disciples: *"Heal the sick, cleanse the lepers, raise the dead, cast out devils: freely you have received, freely give."*

Matthew 10:7-8

And He also told them, *'Behold, I give unto you power to tread on serpents and scorpions, and over all the power of the enemy."*

Luke 10:19

"He that believes on me, the works that I do shall he do also; and greater works than these shall he do."

John 14:12

There have always been many called, but few chosen. As the Apostle Paul wrote: *"This one thing I do, forgetting those things which are behind, and reaching forth unto those things which are before, I press toward the mark for the prize of the high calling of God in Christ Jesus."*

Philippians 3:13-14

God often prepares such vessels for many years, largely hidden from view, before unleashing them upon the world. Then suddenly they appear as if from nowhere, to bring glory to God, to route the devil in His name, and to raise His standard in the earth once again. From such "mighty men and women of valor," Great Revivals are born!

Revival began after the lean spiritual years of World War II; two major national movements revitalized the American church during the Post War era. One was the *Evangelical Awakening Movement* spearheaded by Billy Graham, and the other was the *Healing Revival* represented by William Branham, Oral Roberts, and a host of other lesser-known ministries like A. A. Allen and Jack Coe.

I heard a lot about these revivals from my Grandparents, Vernon and Pearl Derrick, that attended these meetings underneath the big Gospel tents. "Tent Meetings" were held all across the country from 1947-57, and thousands attended these meetings. It was this era that saw the emergence of major evangelists in America.

Revivals intensified in the summer of 1948 with the miraculous prophetic restoration of the State of Israel. In the Bible, Isaiah 66:8 predicted it would happen with a nation being born in a day. The Restoration of the State of Israel was a major prophetic worldly event for all Jews and Christians establishing the first Jewish State in nearly 2,000 years. That may help to explain why so many men received an anointing to evangelize to the unsaved, sick and infirmed with an intense hunger to experience miracles.

Evangelists began to have extraordinary crusades preaching in the "Great Awakening." Billy Graham who preached in the Great Awakening was catapulted to national fame after his Los Angeles campaign in October 1949. Further meetings broadened as massive crowds gathered by the thousands at his crusades.

William Branham is widely regarded as the initiator and the pacesetter of the "Great Healing Revival." Branham's first series of meetings in St Louis' in June 1946 generally mark the inauguration of the modern healing revival. William Branham is the person universally acknowledged as the revival's "father."

The appearance of his miraculous healing campaigns in 1946, including the astonishing use of spiritual gifts (discernment of spirits, the word of knowledge and healing) ignited the dry tinder-box of American Pentecostalism and fanned its flames into a mighty fire of salvation-deliverance Holy Spirit miracle revivals. These miracle revivals were an extraordinary, heaven-sent move of God which revitalized American Pentecostalism, revived the preaching of the *Full Gospel*, and popularized the doctrine of Divine-Healing.

Scores of healing evangelists traversed America and went into the entire world praying for the sick. Thousands were healed, tens of thousands were converted, droves of missionaries were sent to evangelize the masses, churches were planted, and nations were seeded with the Gospel. A result of these major healing ministries was a renewed belief and emphasis in Divine-Healing among many Christians. It was the start of the broader Charismatic Movement, which today numbers about 500 million worldwide.

Oklahoma's own *Oral Roberts* was perhaps the leading figure of the Great Healing Revival movement, and the one to leave the biggest legacy, including the university bearing his name in Tulsa. Many have described Roberts as "one of the most influential religious leaders in the world in the twentieth century." Roberts influenced the course of modern Christianity as profoundly as any American religious leader.

From his beginnings in 1947, and over the next 30 years, he conducted over 300 major healing crusades and personally prayed for over one million people. He traveled across America preaching and praying in the largest tent ever used to promote the gospel.

Another innovation was his national weekly television program which took his healing crusades to millions who had never been exposed to the healing message. His radio program was heard on over 500 stations and served to propagate the message of healing and deliverance. By 1980, he was receiving more than five million letters annually from supporters requesting the prayer of faith.

By the early 1950's, scores of healing evangelists filled tents and auditoriums around the country, attracting tens of thousands of people and reporting thousands of healings and other miracles. There are other names worth mentioning as they formed part of the great mosaic of ministries that made the Great Healing Revival such an effective movement.

A. A. Allen was by far the most important revivalist to emerge in the early days, and he was one of the few that had a substantial following right up to his death in 1970. He was bold and flamboyant with skillful rhetoric and dynamic showmanship. His reporting of miracles, signs, and wonders may have bordered on the sensational, but no one could deny his pulpit presence, his popular appeal, and the amazing power present at his meetings.

Jack Coe was an established evangelist when the revival broke in 1947. He was a large, self-assured man who had a dynamic personality and stage presence. He rented his first tent in 1947 and soon became one of the foremost healing revivalists. In 1951 he purchased what he described as the largest gospel tent in the world from *Ringling Brothers and Barnum & Bailey Circus*, seating 22,000 people. His was the only ministry that seriously challenged Oral Roberts as the popular leader of the revival. Coe had an ability to present the Gospel with unusual power. When praying for the sick, he was full of faith and boldness, often looking for the hardest cases.

A few of the healing evangelists specialized in foreign evangelism, but many of the independent ministers of the 1950s conducted crusades outside the United States, attracting hundreds of thousands to healing revivals in Latin America, Africa, and Asia. Scores of extraordinary revivals led by other evangelists such as R.W. Shambach, Rex Humbard, T.L. Lowery, Tommy Hicks, T.L. Osborn, William Freeman, Velmer Gardner, Franklin Hall, David Nunn and W. V. Grant, enjoyed considerable success in the healing realm. Later, Lester Sumrall and Morris Cerullo would take up their batons with a vision for world evangelization.

It is generally accepted that these revivals peaked by 1957, but its impact and influence extended far into the next few decades, as its main message and ministry became absorbed by the ever-increasing Pentecostal and Charismatic churches across the world.

UNITED STATES PRESIDENTIAL ELECTION OF 1948

"I will bless those who bless you, and curse those who curse you: and in thee shall all families of the earth be blessed."

Genesis 12:3

"And he changeth the times and the seasons: he removeth kings, and setteth up kings: he giveth wisdom unto the wise, and knowledge to them that know understanding. He revealeth the deep and secret things: he knoweth what is in the darkness, and the light dwelleth with him."

Daniel 2:21-22

God sits on His throne with complete control of the universe. For His purpose, He removes kings and sets up kings. Let's look back in history to the presidential election of 1948 by examining an example of God's divine control and where He blessed those who blessed Israel. God reminds us in Isaiah 45:1 that He keeps His promises. *"They are His appointed, whose right hand I have holden."* Let's continue in this section to review how He kept His promise.

In the presidential election of 1948, incumbent President Harry S. Truman, the Democratic nominee, who had succeeded to the presidency after the death of President Franklin D. Roosevelt in 1945, successfully ran for election for a full term against Thomas E. Dewey, the Republican nominee.

Given Truman's sinking popularity and the seemingly fatal three-way split in the Democratic Party, Dewey appeared unbeatable. Top Republicans believed that all their candidate had to do to win was to avoid major mistakes; in keeping with this advice, Dewey carefully avoided risks. He spoke in platitudes, avoided controversial issues, and was vague on what he planned to do as president. Speech after speech was filled with non-political, optimistic assertions of the obvious, including the now infamous quote, "You know that your future is still ahead of you."

57

An editorial in <u>The (Louisville) Courier-Journal</u> summed it up as such: "No presidential candidate in the future will be so inept that four of his major speeches can be boiled down to these historic four sentences:

Agriculture is important. Our rivers are full of fish. You cannot have freedom without liberty. Our future lies ahead." Truman, trailing in the polls, decided to adopt a slashing, no-holds-barred campaign. He ridiculed Dewey by name, criticized Dewey's refusal to address specific issues, and scornfully targeted the Republican-controlled 80th Congress with a wave of relentless and blistering partisan assaults.

Truman nicknamed the Republican-controlled Congress as the "do-nothing," a remark which brought strong criticism from Republican Congressional leaders, however, brought no comment from Dewey. In fact, Dewey rarely mentioned Truman's name during the campaign, which fit into his strategy of appearing to be above petty partisan politics.

The 80th Congress played into Truman's hands, delivering very little in the way of substantive legislation during this time. Truman simply ignored the fact that Dewey's policies were considerably more liberal than most of his fellow Republicans, and instead, he concentrated his fire against the obstructionist tendencies of the unpopular 80th Congress. When discussing the 80th Congress, Truman said, "No man should be allowed to be the President who does not understand hogs or hasn't been around a manure pile."

Truman toured much of the nation with his "fiery rhetoric," playing to large, enthusiastic crowds. "Give 'em hell, Harry" was a popular slogan shouted out at stop after stop along the tour. The polls and the pundits, however, all held that Dewey's lead was insurmountable and that Truman's efforts were for naught. Indeed, Truman's own staff considered the campaign a last hurrah. Even Truman's wife Bess had private doubts that her husband could win. The only person who appears to have considered Truman's campaign to be winnable was the president himself, who confidently predicted victory to anyone and everyone who would listen to him.

In the final weeks of the campaign, American movie theaters agreed to play two short newsreel-like campaign films in support of the two major-party candidates; each film had been created by its respective campaign organization. The Dewey film, shot professionally on an impressive budget, featured very high production values, but somehow reinforced an image of the New York governor as cautious and distant.

The Truman film, hastily assembled on virtually no budget by the perpetually cash-short Truman campaign, relied heavily on public-domain and newsreel footage of the president taking part in major world events and signing important legislation. Perhaps unintentionally, the Truman film visually reinforced an image of him as engaged and decisive. Years later, historian David McCullough cited the expensive, but lackluster, Dewey film, and the far cheaper, but more effective, Truman film, as important factors in determining the preferences of undecided voters.

As the campaign drew to a close, the polls showed Truman was gaining. Though Truman lost all nine of the Gallup Poll's post-convention surveys, Dewey's Gallup lead dropped from 17 points in late September, to 9 points in mid-October, to just 5 points by the end of the month with the poll's margin of error.

Although Truman was gaining momentum, most political analysts were reluctant to break with the conventional wisdom and say that a Truman victory was a serious possibility. In September, nearly two months before Election Day, pollster *Elmo Roper*, of Roper Research Associates announced, "Thomas E. Dewey is almost as good as elected. I can think of nothing duller or more intellectually barren than acting like a sports announcer who feels he must pretend he is witnessing a neck-and-neck race." Roper stopped polling voters until the final week before the election when he took another poll. It showed "a slight shift" to Truman, it still gave Dewey a heavy lead, however, so he decided not to hedge his bet.

In the campaign's final days, many in the media, newspapers, magazines, and political pundits were so confident of Dewey's impending victory they wrote articles to be printed the morning after the election speculating about the new "Dewey Presidency." Life Magazine printed a large photo in its final edition before the election. Entitled "Our Next President Rides by Ferryboat over San Francisco Bay," the photo showed Dewey and his staff riding across the city's harbor.

Newsweek polled fifty experts; all fifty predicted a Dewey win. Several well-known and influential newspaper columnists, such as *Drew Pearson* and *Joseph Alsop*, wrote columns to be printed the morning after the election speculating about Dewey's possible choices for his cabinet. The day before the election, Pearson wrote that Truman's election was "impossible."

Famous New York City newspaper columnist, *Walter Winchell* reported that gambling odds were 15 to 1 against Truman. More than 500 newspapers, accounting for over 78% of the nation's total circulation, endorsed Dewey. Truman picked up 182 endorsements, accounting for just 10% of America's newspaper readership. *Alistair Cooke*, the distinguished writer for the Manchester Guardian newspaper in the United Kingdom, published an article on the day of the election entitled, "Harry S. Truman: A Study of a Failure."

For its television coverage, NBC News constructed a large cardboard model of the White House containing two elephants that would pop out when NBC announced Dewey's victory; since Truman's defeat was considered certain, no donkeys were placed in the White House model. As Truman made his way to his hometown of Independence, Missouri, to await the election returns, some among his inner circle had already accepted other jobs, and not a single reporter traveling on his campaign train thought that he would win.

On election night, Dewey, his family, and campaign staff confidently gathered in the *Roosevelt Hotel* in New York City to await the returns. Truman, aided by the Secret Service, sneaked away from reporters covering him in Kansas City and rode to nearby Excelsior Springs, Missouri. There he took a room in the historic *Elms Hotel*, had dinner and a Turkish bath, and went to sleep. As the votes came in, Truman took an early lead that he never lost.

The election is considered to be the greatest election upset in American history. Virtually every prediction (with or without public opinion polls) indicated that Truman would be defeated by Dewey. Truman's feisty campaign style energized his base of traditional Democrats, consisting of most of the white South; as well he received a record number of Catholic and Jewish voters; he also surprisingly fared well with Midwestern farmers. The election results totaled Truman with 49.55% of the popular vote to Dewey's 45.07%. In the Electoral College, Truman amassed 303 votes by winning 28 states, while Dewey captured 189 electoral votes by winning 16 states.

Part of the reason Truman's victory came as such a shock was because of the uncorrected flaws in the emerging craft of public opinion polling. They didn't poll or factor in the common rural American. According to historian *William Manchester*, "many professional pollsters believed in what some had come to call *Farley's Law*." After his sensational prediction in 1936, Farley had said that in his opinion, voters made up their minds during conventions; the campaigns, he implied, were ineffective carnivals." Manchester added that "the pollster's greatest blunder, however, was their indifference to the last-minute impact of Truman's great effort."

Gallup's September 24th report foresaw 46.5% for Dewey to 38% for Truman. Gallup's last column, appearing in the Sunday papers two days before the election, showed Truman gaining sharply, to 44% and the interviews on which it was based had been conducted two weeks earlier. The national mood was shifting daily, almost hourly. After the election, a study by the University of Michigan revealed that "14% of Truman's voters had decided to vote for him in the last fortnight of the campaign." Gallup and Roper also analyzed the votes. They learned that one voter in every seven made up his mind in the last two weeks before the election. Of these, 75 percent picked Truman, which was more than his margin of victory.

Other possible factors for Truman's victory included his aggressive, populist campaign style, Dewey's complacent, distant approach to the campaign, and his failure to respond to Truman's attacks. Broad public approval of Truman's foreign policy, notably the Berlin Airlift of that year, and widespread dissatisfaction with the institution Truman labeled as the "do-nothing, good-for-nothing 80th Republican Congress" are other factors that led to his win over Dewey.

In addition, after suffering a relatively severe recession in 1946 and 1947, where both unemployment and inflation rose, heightening fears that the nation's post-war economic boom was over. The economy began recovering throughout 1948, thus possibly motivating many voters to give Truman credit for the economic recovery.

After his re-election victory, Truman's economic policy sought to balance the federal budget; any budget surplus would be applied to the national debt. As the economy stalled, Truman in mid-1949 abandoned his hope for a balanced budget and gave some "tax breaks" to businesses.

The economy responded under President Truman; the United States enjoyed a post–World War II economic expansion boom. It was a period of economic prosperity like never before seen. Immediately after the establishment of Israel, according to the *United States Bureau of Economic Analysis*, the Gross Domestic Product (GDP) the annual growth rate average for the United States from 1948-52 was 4.90%. The highest quarterly growth rate and still a record was the first quarter of 1950, at an amazing 16.90%.

The blessings of the United States directly connect to God on how we treat Israel. The rebirthing of the Jewish State of Israel in 1948 was helped by scripture loving President Harry S. Truman. He persuaded the United Nations to recognize Israel as a nation and God rewarded him with a Win in the presidential election. Since 1948, the United States has contributed billions of dollars in aid to Israel.

One of the United States' most worthwhile accomplishments has been its consistent regard for the plight of the Jewish Nation. Since the discovery of America by Christopher Columbus and the founding of the United States, no nation in the history of the world has a better record of treating individual Jews with respect than does America. The same can be said for our befriending Israel as a nation. America has committed many sins for which we may well deserve judgment, but as a nation, we have been a consistent friend of the Jews and the State of Israel, as well as a benefactor.

America's strong bonds with Israel are well-known. These bonds are unbreakable. It is based on cultural and historical ties and the recognition that the aspiration for a Jewish Homeland is rooted in a tragic history that cannot be denied. There is no doubt America has indeed been blessed because we have blessed Israel since her founding in 1948.

"The Lord is good, a stronghold in the day of trouble; and He knoweth them that trust in Him."

Nahum 1:7

"Therefore, my beloved brethren, be ye steadfast, unmovable, always abounding in the work of the Lord, forasmuch as ye know that your labor is not in vain in the Lord."

1 Corinthians 15:58

THE FOUR BLOOD MOON TETRAD OF 1967-68

The Four Blood Moon Tetrad of 1967-68 was the *"second"* tetrad after the founding of the United States and Israel. It occurred just after Israel recaptured Jerusalem after the Six-Day War-another prophetic biblical event. Winning the war marked the reunification and annexing of East Jerusalem as the capital of the Jewish State of Israel for the first time in nearly 2,000 years. The Six-Day War, also known as the 1967 Arab–Israeli War, was fought between June 5 and 10, 1967 by Israel and the neighboring states of Egypt, Jordan, and Syria.

Outnumbered and underequipped, Israel's pre-war estimates of causalities would range from 10,000 to total annihilation. Opposing the small nation was a sizable coalition of forces, supported and supplied primarily by the Soviet Union. This combined army stood strong at roughly 465,000 troops, 2,880 tanks, and 900 aircraft compared to Israel's 264,000 soldiers, 800 tanks, and 300 aircraft.

In the period leading up to June 1967, tensions became dangerously heightened. Days before the war, Egyptian President *Gamal Abdel Nasser* declared, "The armies of Egypt, Jordan, Syria, and Lebanon are poised on the borders of Israel...to face the challenge, while standing behind us are the armies of Iraq, Algeria, Kuwait, Sudan and the whole Arab nation. This act will astound the world. Today they will know that the Arabs are arranged for battle, the critical hour has arrived. We have reached the stage of serious action and not declarations."

In reaction to the mobilization of Egyptian forces along the Israeli border in the Sinai Peninsula, Israel launched a series of preemptive airstrikes against Egyptian airfields. The Egyptians were caught by surprise, and nearly the entire Egyptian air force was destroyed with few Israeli losses, giving the Israelis air superiority. Simultaneously, the Israelis launched a ground offensive into the Gaza Strip and the Sinai, which again caught the Egyptians by surprise. After some initial resistance, President

Nasser ordered the evacuation of the Sinai. Israeli forces rushed westward in pursuit of the Egyptians, inflicted heavy losses, and conquered the Sinai.

President Nasser induced Syria and Jordan to begin attacks on Israel by using the initially confused situation to claim that Egypt had defeated the Israeli air strike. Jordan was reluctant to enter the war. President Nasser used the confusion of the first hours of the conflict to convince *King Hussein* of Jordan that he was victorious; he claimed as evidence a radar sighting of a squadron of Israeli Aircraft returning from bombing raids in Egypt, which he said was Egyptian aircraft in route to attack Israel.

The Israel Defense Forces (IDF's) strategic plan was to remain on the defensive along the Jordanian front, to enable focus in the expected campaign against Egypt. Under orders from *General Narkis*, the Israelis responded only with small-arms fire, firing in a flat trajectory to avoid hitting civilians, holy sites, or the Old City.

On June 5th, the Jordanian Army began shelling Israel. Soon after a message was sent to King Hussein by IDF Command promising not to initiate any action against Jordan if it stayed out of the war. King Hussein replied that it was too late, "the die was cast."

At 11:15 am, Jordanian howitzers began a 6,000-shell barrage at Israeli Jerusalem. The Jordanians initially targeted *Kibbutz Ramat Rachel* in the south and *Mount Scopus* in the north, then ranged into the city center and outlying neighborhoods. Military installations, the Prime Minister's Residence, and the *Knesset Compound* were also targeted. Israeli civilian casualties totaled 20 dead and about 1,000 wounded. Some 900 buildings were damaged.

On June 7, 1967, near the Old City, heavy fighting ensued. The IDF Commander had ordered troops not to enter the Old City; however, upon hearing that the United Nations was about to declare a ceasefire, the IDF Commander changed his mind, and without cabinet clearance, decided to counterattack and capture it.

Two Paratroop Battalions attacked *Augusta-Victoria Hill*, high ground overlooking the Old City from the east. One battalion attacked from Mount Scopus, and another attacked from the valley between it and the Old City. Another paratroop battalion broke into the Old City, and was joined by the other two battalions after their missions were complete. The paratroopers met little resistance; the Israelis did not use armor during the battle out of fear of severe damage to the Old City.

As the Israeli army entered the ancient City of Jerusalem, and liberated the *Temple Mount* and the *Western Wall* after the Old City fell, *Rabbi Shlomo Goren*, Chief Rabbi of the Military Rabbinate of the IDF, with a "trump", sounded his shofar while clutching a Torah at the base of the Western Wall. The ancient holy capital city, west and east Jerusalem unified under complete Jewish control for the first time in since 70 AD. Israeli counterattacks resulted in the seizure of East Jerusalem as well as the West Bank from the Jordanians, while Israel's retaliation against Syria resulted in its occupation of the *Golan Heights*.

The Jerusalem Brigade reinforced the paratroopers, and continued to the south, capturing Judea and Gush Etzion. Hebron was taken without any resistance. Israeli forces continued and seized Bethlehem, taking the city after a brief battle that left some 40 Jordanian soldiers dead, with the remainder fleeing.

By June 10th, Israel had completed its final offensive in the Golan Heights, and a ceasefire was signed the day after. Israel had seized the Gaza Strip, the Sinai Peninsula, the West Bank of the Jordan River including East Jerusalem and the Golan Heights. Overall, Israel's territory grew by a factor of three, including about one million Arabs placed under Israel's direct control in the newly captured territories. Israel's strategic depth grew to at least 300 kilometers in the south, 60 kilometers in the east, and 20 kilometers of extremely rugged terrain in the north, a security asset that would prove useful in the *Yom Kippur War* six years later.

America's role in the 1967 war was influenced by its earlier involvement. The Americans also sponsored a United Nations resolution establishing the United Nations Emergency Force presence between the Egyptians and the Israelis. During the run-up to the Six-Day War, the Americans repeatedly rebuffed Israeli requests for military aid and approval for an Israeli preemptive attack on Egypt.

The United States was bogged down in Vietnam and facing domestic opposition and protests to the war. The administration was disdained to become embroiled in a second front. Rather than get involved militarily, the Americans aggressively pursued diplomatic solutions and sought to cobble together an international regatta to challenge the Egyptian blockade on Israeli shipping in the *Straits of Tiran*, a campaign that ultimately failed.

The United States continued to refuse to aid Israel militarily. The American opposition to unilateral Israeli action began to soften in the beginning of June 1967. President Lyndon Johnson continued to caution Israel against preemption. A number of the President's advisors had concluded that the United States interests would be best served by Israel "going it alone," and by this time the Israelis did so.

This leads us back to the setting of 1967, the Six-Day War, and the Presence of God. The God of Israel indeed is still in control of human events. Satan has tried to obstruct the plan of God since creation by attempting to wipe God's chosen people off the face of the earth. The civilizations and empires of the Assyrians, Aztecs, Egyptians, Mongols, and the Spartans no longer exist, but the Jewish people thrive to this day.

Israel was not destroyed by overwhelming odds in 1967. Instead, in a matter of six days, facing four competent armies, the small nation miraculously quadrupled its land and retook many holy sites including Jerusalem and the Temple Mount. Israel reported 760 casualties, while the Arab deaths hover somewhere around 18,000 men. The conflict is filled with many first-hand accounts of awe-inspiring happenings that are hard to explain even today and bring to mind the scripture.

"But all who devour you will be devoured; all your enemies will go into exile. Those who plunder you will be plundered; all who make spoil of you I will despoil. But I will restore you to health and heal your wounds,' declares the LORD, 'because you are called an outcast, Zion for whom no one cares."

Jeremiah 30: 16-17

Scriptures characterize how much of the world will hate the Jews. The world secretly detests God's people and especially envies Judah because they have been visibly blessed and protected by God. This is obvious when you see many of the miracles performed, that as a whole, cannot explained by any other logical force than God's protection of his people and His Holy Land.

SECOND SPIRITUAL OUTPOURING:
THE CHARISMATIC MOVEMENT

Let's start again with another look at the Four Blood Moon Tetrad of 1967-68, to build further on the spiritual connection between Israel, and America. I suggest we can determine by looking back at this period and reexamine history; that this was indeed God's *"Second Major Wave of Rain"* of an outpouring of the Holy Spirit in America. Revival began after the Four Blood Moon Tetrad, which was coupled with another prophetic biblical fulfilment, the restoration event in Israel which occurred with the reunification of Jerusalem.

In June of 1967, the Six-Day War victory marked the reunification and annexing of East Jerusalem as the capital of the Jewish State of Israel for the first time in nearly 2,000 years. This was another major prophetic restoration event worldwide for Jews and Christians. This could help to explain the stimulation that started the *Catholic Charismatic Renewal* of 1967 at Duquesne University in Pittsburgh, Pennsylvania. The movement led to the creation of many independent evangelical charismatic churches more in tune with this revival of the Holy Spirit.

The Catholic Charismatic Renewal dates itself from February 18, 1967. It was on that day when a number of Duquesne University students experienced *Baptism of the Holy Spirit* during a weekend retreat at *The Ark* and *The Dove Retreat Center* near Pittsburgh. Very quickly after that, through contacts of friends and campus ministers, this experience of *Baptism in the Holy Spirit* spread to Notre Dame University, Michigan State University, and the University of Michigan.

In a series of prayer meetings and hastily put together conferences, the experience was shared across the United States in hundreds of locations by the end of 1967. In one conference, a prophecy was given that *Baptism in the Holy Spirit* would go across the nation *"like lightning from coast to coast"* and certainly in that year it seemed to happen.

Examining church history, we find that before 1955, the religious mainstream denominations did not embrace Pentecostal doctrinal beliefs. If a church member or clergyman openly expressed Pentecostalism or other such views, a member would either voluntarily or involuntarily separate from their existing denomination. The Charismatic Movement from 1967-73 represented a reversal of this previous pattern, as those influenced by Pentecostal spirituality chose to remain in their original denominations.

The high church wing of the American Episcopal Church became the first traditional ecclesiastical organization to feel the impact of the new movement. Charismatic Christians believe that the gifts of the Holy Spirit, as described in the New Testament, are available to contemporary Christians through the infilling or *Baptism of the Holy Spirit,* with or without the laying on of hands. These spiritual gifts are believed to be manifest in the form of signs, miracles, and wonders, including, but not limited to, speaking in tongues, interpretation, prophecy, healing, and discernment of spirits.

While Pentecostals and Charismatics both share these beliefs, there are differences among the two groups. Many in the Charismatic Movement deliberately distanced themselves from Pentecostalism for cultural and theological reasons. Foremost among theological reasons is the tendency of many Pentecostals to insist that speaking in tongues is always the initial physical sign of receiving Spirit Baptism.

Although specific teachings will vary from group to group, Charismatics generally believe that the *Baptism of the Holy Spirit* occurs at the new birth and prefer to call subsequent encounters with the Holy Spirit by another name, such as being filled with the spirit. In contrast to Pentecostals, Charismatics tend to accept a range of supernatural experiences such as prophecy, miracles, healing, or physical manifestations of an altered state of consciousness, as evidence of having been baptized or filled with the Holy Spirit.

Pentecostals are also distinguished from the Charismatic Movement on the basis of style of worship and outreach. Also, Pentecostals have traditionally placed a high value on evangelization and missionary work. Charismatics, on the other hand, have tended to see their movement as a force for revitalization and renewal within their own church traditions.

The most recognized move in the Charismatic Movement was during the "Summer of Love" in 1969, as the decade came to a close and our nation fell on hard times. Those of my parents' age can never forget the dark days of the 1960's, when it seemed that an entire generation, "Turned On, tuned in, and dropped out," as *Timothy Leary* put it. Racial conflict illuminated in the Southern United States as both *Dr. Martin Luther King Jr.* and *Robert Kennedy* were assassinated. Racial riots and war protests erupted in our city streets as the Vietnam War tore at the fabric of our nation. Corruption in Washington D.C's *Watergate* scandal later sent our politics into chaos.

The disillusioned long-haired youth, "hippies" adopted *countercultural* values and protested the *establishment*. This emerging youth culture of the distressed centered in San Francisco's *Haight-Ashbury District*. Hallucinogenic drugs, long hair, short-skirts, tie-dyed clothes, and eastern mysticism-meditation consumed a generation. The summer commenced with the *Woodstock Festival* in a small town in New York before an audience of 400,000 people. It is widely regarded as the pivotal moment in popular music history, as well as the definitive summit of the counterculture generation. America's youth were desperate and broken. They had become corrupt, both morally and spiritually.

Throughout history, when clouds have hung the lowest, when sin has seemed blackest and faith has been the weakest, there have always been a faithful few elect and remnant who have not sold out nor bowed knee to the devil. They have feared the LORD, called upon his Name, and have not forsaken the assembling of themselves together. These have besought the LORD to revive His work in the midst of the years, and in the midst of fears and tears. God has always answered, filling each heart with love and rekindling each soul with fire from above.

It is amazing what God can do with one couple to spread the word. At the height of the counterculture rebellion, one San Francisco couple, *Ted and Liz Wise*, were feeling a spiritual impulse, but each for a different reason. Ted, a Navy veteran and sailmaker, was interested in the possibility of a spiritual release from what had become for him an out-of-control involvement with the drug LSD. Liz began attending a local church in search of her childhood religious roots in order to be a positive influence for the couple's two children. Before long the Wises became Christians, and as Ted recovered from his earlier drug abuse, the couple began sharing their newfound faith with their friends.

Soon, they rented a farmhouse in northern Marin County, California which they opened as a communal living space shared with three other young Christian couples and their children. They formed what is considered the first community of the fledgling "Jesus Movement." The Jesus Movement also gave birth to the modern Messianic Movement.

Before 1967, there was not a single Messianic congregation in the world. More than a 100 exist today in Israel alone with thousands of Jews in the United States serving *Yeshua*. As the glory in Zion, more Jewish people have come to faith in *Yeshua* in the last generation than at any time since the first century. God is opening the long-blinded eyes and softening the hearts of thousands of Jews just as the Scriptures promised in Romans 11:25-26.

The Wises and other couples also formed the "House of Acts" community and provided the leadership for opening the first "Jesus coffeehouse" in the Haight-Ashbury district, called the "Living Room." They ministered to the street people of the district for the next year and a half. The Living Room ministry, like the House of Acts, became "a greenhouse of fertile Christian ideas and growth" to the blossoming community. Soon coffeehouses opened up and down the West Coast, and the winds of revival began to sweep thousands of hippies to be baptized who were later called "Jesus People."

Further up the Pacific coast in Seattle, Washington, a young Iowa farm girl named Linda Meissner was organizing local teens to form a "Jesus People Army" after leaving Central Bible College, an Assembly of God school in Springfield, Missouri. Meissner's group organized quickly, and one of the early Movement newspapers, "Agape," began under her leadership.

Also in Seattle, the Catacombs, a "Jesus People" coffeehouse, opened in 1969 near the Space Needle. Two Jesus People commune houses, the House of Caleb and House of Esther, were opened in the Wallingford neighborhood of Seattle's North End, a ministry to Seattle's street youth similar in concept to the Living Room in Haight-Ashbury.

Many Christians initially viewed "Jesus People" with skepticism, but on January 1, 1971, the Reverend Billy Graham rode through Pasadena as grand marshal of the Tournament of Roses Parade. A heap of newly converted hippies surrounded him, pointing index fingers toward heaven and shouting, "One Way." Deeply moved, Graham encouraged these young youth who were seeking Jesus Christ out of despair. He called them, "the Jesus Generation" and wrote a book by the same title.

In 1971, "Jesus Christ Superstar," a rock opera with music by *Andrew Lloyd Webber* made its premier in New York on Broadway. A film adaptation of "Jesus Christ Superstar" was released in 1973 and was the eighth highest-grossing film of that year.

Time Magazine featured a purple Jesus on its cover, encircled by a rainbow bearing the words, "the Jesus Revolution." The magazine described Jesus as the "notorious leader" of an underground liberation movement," who bore the appearance of a "typical hippie" with long hair, beard, robe, and wore sandals. He was changing lives, as thousands of "Jesus Freaks" were flooding churches.

Congregations welcomed the unconventional converts and encouraged them to play their guitars, enjoy their folk-rock sound, and write new songs to the LORD, nurturing the emergence of praise and worship music. Ripples of the outpouring spread into youth groups and churches around the world. In 1972, a six-day expo in Dallas, Texas attracted eighty thousand young people.

Their passion for Jesus has never dimmed as yesterday's "Jesus People" are today's church leaders. Fueled by the revival of those days, an army of Christian workers has labored on mission fields for a generation. Many have advanced the cause of Jesus on university campuses and in churches around the world, adding fresh notes to our traditional hymns and giving us a new era of Christian music.

Perhaps the most important legacy of the "Jesus Movement" was its return to the simple Gospel. Jesus says in Matthew 11:30, *"For my yoke is easy, and my burden is light."* New Testament Christianity centers on the life and teachings of Jesus Christ, placing an emphasis on a personal relationship with Him and profession of faith, and are not subject to Old Testament ordinances. The "yoke" is an allusion to the Law of Moses and a "burden" refers to the very heavy ordinances the Scribes and Pharisees lay upon the shoulders of the people, obliging them to a strict observance of them.

Other ministries during the Charismatic Movement trace their rapid rise and beginning to this time period. They took the message of salvation to the airways via television to reach the world. Jim Bakker, Kenneth Copeland, Paul Crouch, Jesse Duplantis, John Hagee, Kenneth Hagin, Hal Lindsey, Pat Robertson, and Jimmy Swaggart were and continue to be significant to this movement. In 2011, a study by a popular Christian magazine showed that almost 500,000,000 people worldwide, or 14 percent of the world's self-identified Christian population, are part of the Charismatic Movement. That's 500 million people, and their impact on Christianity and God's global mission has been powerful and far-reaching.

UNITED STATES PRESIDENTIAL ELECTION OF 1968

I suggest America's refusal and neutrality by its administration not to help Israel during the Six-Day War in 1967 heavenly influenced the United States presidential election of 1968. This will help to explain how God removes kings and sets up kings for His purpose (Daniel 2:21-22).

Incumbent President Lyndon B. Johnson, who had won a landslide victory for the Democratic Party four years earlier, declined not to seek election amid growing protests over the Vietnam War. The election year was boisterous; it was marked by the assassination of civil rights leader Martin Luther King, Jr. and the assassination of Democratic presidential candidate Robert F. Kennedy.

Widespread opposition to the War in Vietnam caused subsequent race riots across the nation. The Black Panther Party, a Revolutionary Black Nationalist, and Socialist organization, organized in October of 1966. The Black Panther Party's core practice was its armed citizens' patrols to monitor the behavior of police officers and challenge police brutality in Oakland, California. Growth of the party grew as killings and arrests of Panthers increased support for the party within the black community and also on the broad political left, both of whom valued the Panthers as a powerful force.

The 1968 Democratic National Convention in Chicago was a scene of violent confrontations between police and anti-war protesters as the Democrats split into multiple factions. Thousands of young activists from around the nation gathered in the city to protest the Vietnam War. On the evening of August 28, in a clash which was covered on live television, Americans were shocked to see Chicago police brutally beating anti-war protesters in the streets of Chicago in front of the *Conrad Hilton Hotel*.

While the protesters chanted "the whole world is watching," the police used clubs and tear gas to beat back or arrest the protesters, leaving many of them bloody and dazed. The police said that their actions were justified because numerous police officers were being injured by bottles, rocks, and broken glass that were being thrown at them by the protestors. The protestors had also yelled verbal insults at the police, calling them "pigs" and other epithets.

The anti-war and police riot divided the Democratic Party's base: some supported the protestors and felt that the police were being heavy-handed, but others disapproved of the violence and supported the police. Meanwhile, the convention itself was marred by the strong-arm tactics of Chicago's mayor *Richard J. Daley* (who was seen on television angrily cursing Senator *Abraham Ribicoff* from Connecticut and had made a speech at the convention denouncing the excesses of the Chicago police). In the end, the nomination itself was anti-climactic, with Vice-President Humphrey, handily beating McCarthy and McGovern on the first ballot.

The Republican nominee, former Vice President Richard Nixon, narrowly won the 1968 popular vote by 0.7% over the Democratic nominee, incumbent Vice President Hubert Humphrey, but he easily won the electoral college 301 - 191.

President Nixon again ran for re-election in 1972, emphasizing a good economy and his successes in foreign affairs. Nixon ended American involvement in the war in Vietnam in 1973 and brought the American POW's home, and ended the military draft. Nixon's visit to the People's Republic of China in 1972 opened diplomatic relations between the two nations, and he initiated the Anti-Ballistic Missile Treaty with the Soviet Union the same year.

Nixon easily won the 1972 election in a landslide. Overall, Nixon won 60.7% of the popular vote. No candidate since has managed to equal or surpass Nixon's total percentage or margin of the popular vote, and his electoral vote total and percentage has been surpassed only once. His state total was matched only once by Ronald Reagan in 1984.

Nixon's mother was a Quaker, and his father converted from Methodism to the Quaker faith. As a young boy growing up in California, his mother spoke over him a prophetic word that one day he would be in a powerful position, and a situation would arise where Israel and the Jews needed his help. Nixon's upbringing was marked by evangelical Quaker observances of the time, such as refraining from alcohol, dancing, and swearing.

Nixon's early life was marked by hardship, and he later quoted as saying to describe his boyhood, "We were poor, but the glory of it was we didn't know it."

While President, Nixon's Middle Eastern policy was that the United States would avoid direct combat assistance to allies where possible, instead giving them assistance to defend themselves. The United States greatly increased arms sales to the Middle East, particularly Israel, Iran and Saudi Arabia during the Nixon Administration. The Nixon Administration strongly supported Israel, an American ally in the Middle East.

Since the reestablishment of Israel in 1948, a series of regional conflicts, often including violent fighting, had broken out between Israel and the Arab States. The Six-Day War of 1967 was one of them, and it resulted in a decisive Israeli victory, gaining new boundaries for Israel. Syria and Egypt, two leading nations in the Arab world, in a summit after The Six-Day War, declared there would be "no peace, no recognition, and no negotiation with Israel." Egyptian President Anwar Sadat publicly decried the Jewish State.

On October 6, 1973, a coordinated surprise attack occurred against Israel on *Yom Kippur*. Israel could not have been more vulnerable, on the holiest of all days on the Jewish calendar, a time when the entire nation comes to a virtual standstill (much like Christmas Day in America). Even non-observant Jews honor this holyday by fasting, staying home or going to synagogue, and refraining from the use of fire, electricity, and communications systems. There had been concern about possible attacks, but until just shortly before the attacks began, Israeli intelligence was not able to determine conclusively that an attack was imminent.

Israeli tanks, which numbered about 180, faced over 1,400 Syrian tanks. At the Suez Canal, a mere 436 Israeli infantry were poised to fight over 80,000 Egyptian soldiers. The attacks by Egypt and Syria were backed by nine Arab states, as well as the Soviet Union. The situation for Israel did not look promising for survival.

By the second day, the slaughtering of Israeli troops and destruction of their equipment had been such a blow, *Moshe Dayan*, the Minister of Defense, the hero in the Six-Day War, started talking about pulling back and even possible surrender. *Golda Meir*, Prime Minister of Israel, resisted this, but she did have an aid secure a lethal pill from her doctor. Just in case her Arab enemies prevailed, Meir would take her own life. Prime Minister, Golda Meir was known for her stalwartness, her iron will, and inflexible nature.

As a result, Israel did not surrender. The reserve troops approached the front lines, and the tide slowly began to turn in Israel's favor, but, arms and ammunition supplies were dangerously low. The Arab threats of an oil embargo and trade boycott had effectively halted European munitions re-supply, so Meir turned her attention to the United States and the Nixon Administration.

United States Secretary of State *Henry Kissinger* and Meir's relationship was to say the least a bit rocky. When Golda Meir first asked for assistance, Kissinger's reported response was to let Israel "bleed a little." Not to be discouraged, at 3 a.m. on the second day, Golda Meir picked up the phone and personally called President Richard Nixon and asked for help. It is reported that Nixon heard the prophetic word from when he was a young boy and the voice of his Quaker mother as he listened to Meir. By the time she hung up, Golda Meir had the weapons needed to help her country that swung the pendulum in Israel's favor.

Israel suffered heavy losses, and Nixon ordered an airlift to resupply Israeli losses, cutting through inter-departmental squabbles and bureaucracy and taking personal responsibility for any response by Arab nations. America's resupply included 815 total aircraft sorties, bringing Israel 56 combat aircraft and 27,900 tons of munitions and supplies. Both Secretary of State Kissinger and President Nixon wanted to conduct the airlift, but according to the CIA director, "Nixon gave it the greater sense of urgency." He said, "You get the stuff to Israel! Now! Now! Now!"

More than a week later, by the time the United States and the Soviet Union began negotiating a truce, Israel had penetrated deep into enemy territory. When *Soviet Premier Brezhnev* threatened unilaterally to enforce any peacekeeping mission militarily, Nixon ordered the military to *DEFCON-3*, placing all military personnel and bases on alert for nuclear war. This was the closest that the world had come to nuclear war since the *Cuban Missile Crisis*. Brezhnev backed down as a result of Nixon's actions.

President Richard Nixon to this day is highly regarded in Israel. Meir and Nixon kept in frequent touch throughout the ordeal. For the rest of Meir's life, she referred to Nixon as "my president," and said, "For generations to come, all will be told of the miracle of the immense planes from the United States bringing in the material that meant life to our people."

Israel's victory was largely due to support of the United States. Arab *OPEC* nations retaliated by refusing to sell crude oil to America, resulting in the *1973 oil crisis*. The embargo caused gasoline shortages and rationing in late 1973, and was eventually ended by the oil-producing nations as peace in the Middle East took hold.

After the war and under Nixon's presidency, the United States reestablished relations with Egypt for the first time since 1967. Nixon made one of his final international visits as president to the Middle East in June 1974 and became the first President to visit Israel.

We can only speculate what could have happened to Israel if incumbent President Lyndon B. Johnson had sought and won re-election in 1968. The presidential election of 1972 may have had a much different outcome for the Democrats. Instead, Richard Nixon won office in both 1968 and 1972. God positioned the son of a Quaker into the White House where he answered the call to help the State of Israel and the Jewish people in their most dire need for survival.

God sees the end of all things as clearly as their beginning. God knew that Israel would require future help and allowed a president to be elected that would come to the aid of Israel and her people.

"And he changeth the times and the seasons: he removeth kings, and setteth up kings: he giveth wisdom unto the wise, and knowledge to them that know understanding. He revealeth the deep and secret things: he knoweth what is in the darkness, and the light dwelleth with him."

Daniel 2:21-22

THE FOUR BLOOD MOON TETRAD OF 2014-15

What future events could there be for America with the current Four Blood Moon Tetrad of 2014-15? What connection to God's appointed harvests and seasons is there if any?

Lunar eclipses have always signaled to both ancient and modern man the seasons of harvest. They have also identified God's appointed holy feasts days (Leviticus 23). Harvest seasons of ancient Israel are centered on the *seven feasts* of Israel mentioned in the Bible. Many believers say there is no sign that can be drawn from studying these feasts or lunar eclipses that connect Israel with America, nor do they in their minds foretell patterns of future events. But I think otherwise. Various biblical laws and stories refer to ancient Israelite crops and harvests. It may, therefore, be helpful to have some general information about the God's appointed harvests and their seasons.

Major crops of the land are listed in Deuteronomy 8:8: wheat, barley, grapes, figs, pomegranates, olives, and honey. In ancient Israel, the primary harvest season extended from April to November. This harvest period might be divided into three seasons and three major crops: the spring grain harvest, the summer grape harvest, and the autumn olive harvest. These harvests have a general correspondence with the holy feasts of Israel. Are these feasts a picture of God's appointed plans? Have some of the feasts already been fulfilled prophetically by Jesus and the Church? Could other feasts foretell shadows of future prophetic *set time* events to come?

In a nutshell, here is the prophetic significance of each of the seven appointed feasts of Israel:

1.) Passover (Leviticus 23:5) - Pointed to Jesus Christ as our Passover lamb (1 Corinthians 5:7) whose blood would be shed for our sins. Jesus was crucified on the day of preparation for the Passover at the same hour that the lambs were being slaughtered for the Passover meal that evening (John 19:14).

2.) Unleavened Bread (Leviticus 23:6) - Pointed to Jesus's sinless life (as leaven is a picture of sin in the Bible), making Him the perfect sacrifice for our sins. Jesus' body was in the grave during the first days of this feast, like a kernel of wheat planted and waiting to burst forth as the bread of life.

3.) First Fruits (Leviticus 23:10-14) - Pointed to Jesus's resurrection as the first fruits of the righteous. Jesus was resurrected on this very day, which is one of the reasons that Paul refers to Jesus Christ in 1 Corinthians 15:20 as the "first fruits from the dead."

4.) Weeks or Pentecost (Leviticus 23:16) - Occurred fifty days after the beginning of the Feast of Unleavened Bread and pointed to the great harvest of souls and the gift of the Holy Spirit for both Jew and Gentile, who would be brought into the kingdom of God during the Church Age (see Acts 2). The Church was actually established on this day when God poured out His Holy Spirit, and 3,000 Jews responded to Peter's great sermon and his first proclamation of the gospel.

5.) Trumpets (Leviticus 23:24) - The first of the fall feasts. Many believe this day points to the Rapture of the Church when Jesus Christ will appear in the heavens as He comes for His bride, the Church. The Rapture is listed in scripture with the blowing of a trumpet (1Thessalonians 4:13-18 and 1 Corinthians 15:52).

6.) Day of Atonement (Leviticus 23:27) - Many believe this prophetically points to the day of the Second Coming of Jesus when He will return to earth. That will be the Day of

Atonement for the Jewish remnant when they "look upon Him whom they have pierced," repent of their sins and receive Him as their Messiah (Zechariah 12:10 and Romans 11:1-6, 25-36).

7.) Tabernacles or Booths (Leviticus 23:34) - Many scholars believe that this feast day points to the LORD's promise that He will once again "tabernacle" with His people when He returns to reign over all the world (Micah 4:1-7).

Should Christians celebrate the feast days, "mo'edim" of Israel today? Colossians 2:16-17 tells us, *"Let no man therefore judge you in meat or in drink, or with respect of a holyday, or of the new moon, or of the Sabbath days. Which are a shadow of things to come; but the body is of Christ."*

Christians are not bound to observe the feasts like an Old Testament Jew. While it is not required for Christians to celebrate the feast days, it is beneficial to study them. But the good news is, when we choose to align our lives with the appointed feasts of God, we enter His cycle of blessing. Once we understand these times, we go from decrease to increase. The appointed times of God are not some legalistic burden, but we should not criticize another believer who does or does not observe these special days and feasts as it says in Romans 14:5.

God is beyond time, but because of His love for us, He reaches down and intervenes in time. A big part of walking in God's blessing involves seeing time from God's perspective and understanding how His cycles operate. The appointed feasts were fixed at the beginning and for all time. They have been observed and celebrated for thousands of years. I suggest if they were important in the past, they will are important now. Certainly, it could be beneficial to celebrate these days if it leads one to a greater understanding and appreciation for Jesus's death and resurrection and the future promise of His coming. As Christians, if we choose to celebrate these special days, we should put Jesus in the center of the celebration, as the One who came to fulfill the prophetic significance of each of them.

As we looked back in history, we discovered that many spiritual outpourings have occurred all across the United States to different people at different times. We reviewed previously two examples of *major waves of rain* of outpourings of the Holy Spirit in America. They both occurred near or during the Four Blood Moon Tetrads of 1949-50 and 1967-68 also with major prophetic biblical restoration events in Israel.

The harvests for souls were plentiful; it was the *"set time"* as each revival grew while they crossed America and the globe saving souls for Jesus Christ. Both spiritual revivals started within the youth as God appointed workers *first* with the Great Awaking and Healing Revivals; and *second*, with the Charismatic Movement.

Jesus said in Matthew 9:37-38, *"The harvest is plentiful, but the workers are few. Therefore beseech the LORD of the harvest to send out workers into His harvest."*

I mentioned previously in the summer of 2016, our local church hosted a Prophetess of God, Sister Sharon Fletcher. The following day I had, what I call, a major "Supernatural Revelation" download from the Holy Spirit while driving to Texas. I prayed to God to let the Holy Spirit reveal to me about the end time harvest. I received a funny answer right away in my spirit, **"Son, you can't have a harvest without RAIN."** I smiled and laughed on the inside, because having grown up on a farm, I should have known this. Seeds in the ground need rain in order to emerge before the harvest comes.

When you buy dry seeds at a gardening store, the seeds are dormant, which means they're inactive. All it usually takes to wake them up, though, is just to add water.

In plant biology, seed *germination* starts when a seed is provided with water. The uptake of water by a dry seed is called *imbibition* (imbibition means to drink). As seeds imbibe water, they expand. Once hydrated, a seed will increase its metabolic activity to produce energy for growth. The water causes pressure within the cell to increase, and they are able to enlarge.

As you see in movies of germinating seeds, the first part of the seedling to emerge from the seed coat is the root, called the *radicle*. Eventually, the shoot will also expand and emerge from the seed. The seedling will emerge from soil into the light where it will be able to obtain energy from sunlight. Once a seedling emerges into the light, the plant undergoes dramatic changes and bears leaves.

The three things plants need to grow are light, food and water. Light from the Sun gives the small plant the energy it needs to begin *photosynthesis*. Photosynthesis is the process the plant uses to convert light energy into food. Like all living things, plants need water. Once a seed sends out roots, these roots will deliver water from the soil to the plant. As the plant grows and needs more water, roots will grow longer and stretch farther to find the necessary water in the soil.

Like seeds in the ground, many Christians in America have been spiritually inactive, dry and dormant. Christians also need "light, food, and living water" to grow and bear fruit. Many people have stopped going to church altogether. There was a small stirring of the Spirit for a while before there were corporate consultants who advised easy doctrines and slid into many churches with their *Starbucks* coffee, bagels, seeker-sensitive, and people-pleasing viewpoints that refuse to preach the Cross, the Blood of Jesus, or the *Baptism of the Holy Spirit*.

Cotton Candy Religion, the "Seeker-Sensitive Consumer Church" is failing a generation of church goers by avoiding teaching sections of scripture (Acts 2) out of fear that certain "pockets" will be offended. Jesus Christ understood that we are all sinners in need of being saved, and He sent the comforter (Holy Spirit) to guide us and teach us all things (John 14:26). No brilliant marketing campaign could ever repackage His teaching. Many churches have hidden their true spiritual condition with big ornate buildings, conventions, and conferences. Many pastors revel in the noise of promotion and advertisement. The fame of men has become greater than the fame Jesus Christ.

Many people leave the faith because they are not being spiritually fed and fulfilled. Sometimes they cannot even articulate the reason why they are leaving. The fancy stage, the bright lights, the cool bands, and the video screens, just become noise to them. They may say it's because of the music, the preaching, or the youth and children's programs, but the real reason they may be leaving could be that they are not encountering God anymore like when they were first saved.

Smith Wigglesworth, a British evangelist who was important in the early history of Pentecostalism, had similar experiences where the Holy Spirit kept telling him to come out of dead works and dead churches.

Just add water! The pattern of the Four Blood Moon Tetrad shows rain for America is on its way. The spiritually inactive, dry and dormant church will thirst no longer and will walk in the light. It just needs the rain of "Living water" to quench their thirst, causing them to sprout into *Radicles*!

"O God, thou art my God; early will I seek thee: my soul thirsteth for thee, my flesh longeth for thee in a dry and thirsty land, where no water is."

Psalm 63:1

Jesus said, *"He that believeth on me, as the scripture hath said, out of his belly shall flow rivers of living water."*

John 7:38

"Behold, I will send you Elijah the prophet before the coming of the great and dreadful day of the LORD: And he shall turn the heart of the fathers to the children, and the heart of the children to their fathers, lest I come and smite the earth with a curse."

Malachi 4:5-6

God established a pattern of perfection with the number *three* throughout the Bible, which means completion and unity. The Four Blood Moon Tetrad of 2014-15 was the *third* tetrad since the founding of the United States and the restoration of the State of Israel.

God's tetrad pattern shows an outpouring of the Holy Spirit is coming like the Spirit of Elijah to the sons and daughters to harvest souls for His kingdom (Joel 2:28). I suggest the ***"Third Major Wave of Rain"*** will be summoned after the Four Blood Moon Tetrad of 2014-15 and *after* another major biblical prophetic restoration event in Israel occurs. What could that be? What do the Sons of Issachar Discern? Can you speculate?

I believe this outpouring will break free and break loose those in despair. The shaking will usher in a great revival. As revival spreads, with increased praise and worship like in the days of *David's Tabernacle*, it will provide a richer kingdom experience as individuals use their gifts in the works of the body of Jesus Christ. A true revival always propels a new generation of workers into the Kingdom. Just as Pentecost fueled the first generation of apostles, so every ensuring revival has thrust laborers into a lifetime of ministry. It will awaken the saints and thrust them into mobilization at a level not yet seen in history.

A generation of preachers, teachers, and missionaries will be mobilized throughout the world. It will be the most awesome move of God for His kingdom in human history. The Holy Spirit will carry a powerful apostolic, prophetic, priestly grace that will come upon His people. It will help others come out of their broken lives of hopelessness with a strong deliverance and anointing spirit.

This revival will touch hearts and assist in the process of healing many who have suffered abuses. God's people will be freed to tear down the partitions of incorrect mindsets, the lies of past experiences, and unresolved pain. His people will be free with new life. Heal the sick. They will work with the Holy Spirit, moving mightily in His Glory to save those who have felt as though they have fallen through the cracks of despair.

I asked God out loud in my pick-up truck, "Where are the storm clouds of revival? Where will it rain first?" I sensed the answer immediately through the Holy Spirit, *"There's fire on the mountain! It's raining in the high places!"* I'm not sure what is meant by this yet. What do the Sons of Issachar discern?

Christians have long been praying for revival and restoration. More than ever, revival is indeed possible, and we have the history to prove it. As dire as our present time appears, America has been at a low point before. We are prone to think our days are worse than those that preceded us; American History is blemished with periods of spiritual trouble. Like ancient Israel, our nation has repeatedly sunk to the depths only to be saved from itself by timely seasons of revival. That's the grace of God!

Do your senses tell you rain is coming? Can you discern it Sons of Issachar? In 1967, a youth revival swept across the country, detonating on colleges and in coffeehouses. Just as the Summer of Love changed the landscape of a generation, rumblings have begun and are being poured out into this generation already. We're turning the corner now!

Almost every revolution has started with students on a college or university campus. Throughout history, both bad and good revolutions frequently begin because student-aged young people are hungry for change and willing to lay down their lives for a cause, whether political, social or spiritual. Throughout Christian history, spiritual battles result in spiritual awakenings, and young people are clearly at the center again. Here comes the Tribe of Judah!

However, to sustain a major move of God, it must be comprised of *three* generations, because God is the God of Abraham, Isaac, and Jacob - *three* generations walking together as one generation. We need the wisdom of the older, the resources of the middle, and the zeal of the younger. We will need the *synergy* of all *three* to work together (Issachar, Zebulun, and Judah). Ours is the generation; the joining of the generations is upon us!

God declared the greatest youth outpouring the world has ever seen is coming soon. This is the *set time* for an increase and a fresh anointing for the ministry of God. Now is America's *set time*! This is our purpose that God has intended since our founding. He will lift us up on a high place of victory and peace, for our *set time* has come. He will rise up the Body of Christ to be a carbon copy of David's Tabernacle, with praise and worship. This is the *set time* He has appointed before the foundations of the world. It is His time to favor the Church with speedy answers to prayers prayed years ago.

"And ye shall know that I am in the midst of Israel and that I am the LORD your God, and none else: and my people shall never be ashamed. And it shall come to pass afterward, that I will pour out my spirit upon all flesh; and your sons and your daughters shall prophecy, your old men shall dream dreams, your young men shall see visions."

Joel 2:27-28

THE SABBATH YEAR OF SHEMITAH

The Sabbath year or Shemitah is the seventh year of the agricultural cycle mandated by the Torah for the Land of Israel, still observed in contemporary Judaism.

In ancient Israel, during Shemitah, God commanded a *set time* for the land to lay fallow and all agricultural activity, including plowing, planting, pruning, and harvesting is forbidden by Jewish law. Other cultivation techniques such as watering, fertilizing, weeding, spraying, trimming and mowing may be performed as a preventive measure only, not to improve the growth of trees or other plants. Additionally, any fruits which grow of their own accord are deemed ownerless and may be picked by anyone. All debts were considered forgiven on the last day of the Shemitah at sunset on the Hebrew calendar date, the 29th of Elul.

Many in Israel today still observe Shemitah. The most recent Sabbath year began at *Rosh Hashanah* on September 24, 2014, and ended September 13, 2015. Chapter 25 of the Book of Leviticus promises bountiful harvests to those who observe the Shemitah and describes its observance as a test of religious faith. A Sabbath year is mentioned several times in the Hebrew Bible by name or by its pattern of six years of activity and one of rest.

Book of Exodus: *"You may plant your land for six years and gather its crops. But during the seventh year, you must leave it alone and withdraw from it. The needy among you will then be able to eat just as you do, and whatever is left over can be eaten by wild animals. This also applies to your vineyard and your olive grove."*

Exodus 23:10–11

Book of Leviticus: *"God spoke to Moses at Mount Sinai, telling him to speak to the Israelites and say to them: When you come to the land that I am giving you, the land must be given a rest period, a Sabbath to God. For six years you may plant your fields, prune*

91

your vineyards, and harvest your crops, but the seventh year is a Sabbath of Sabbaths for the land. It is God's Sabbath during which you may not plant your fields, nor prune your vineyards. Do not harvest crops that grow on their own and do not gather the grapes on your unpruned vines, since it is a year of rest for the land. What grows while the land is resting may be eaten by you, by your male and female slaves, and by the employees and resident hands who live with you. All the crops shall be eaten by the domestic and wild animals that are in your land."

Leviticus 25:1–7

Book of Deuteronomy: *"At the end of every seven years, you shall celebrate the remission year. The idea of the remission year is that every creditor shall remit any debt owed by his neighbor and brother when God's remission year comes around. You may collect from the alien, but if you have any claim against your brother for a debt, you must relinquish it."*

Deuteronomy 15:1–6

"Moses then gave them the following commandment: At the end of each seven years, at a fixed time on the festival of Sukkoth, after the year of release, when all Israel comes to present themselves before God your LORD, in the place that He will choose, you must read this Torah before all Israel, so that they will be able to hear it. You must gather together the people, the men, women, children, and proselytes from your settlements, and let them hear it. They will thus learn to be in awe of God your LORD, carefully keeping all the words of this Torah. Their children, who do not know, will listen and learn to be in awe of God your LORD, as long as you live in the land which you are crossing the Jordan to occupy."

Deuteronomy 31:10–13

Book of Jeremiah: *"Thus saith the LORD, the God of Israel: I made a covenant with your fathers in the day that I brought them forth out of the land of Egypt, out of the house of bondage, saying: At the end of seven years ye shall let go every man his brother that is a Hebrew, that hath been sold unto thee, and hath served thee six years, thou shalt let him go free from thee; but your fathers hearkened not unto Me, neither inclined their ear."*

Jeremiah 34:13–14

THE SABBATH YEAR OF JUBILEE

"And ye shall hallow the fiftieth year, and proclaim liberty throughout the land unto all the inhabitants thereof; it shall be a Jubilee unto you; and ye shall return every man unto his possession, and ye shall return every man unto his family."

Leviticus 25:10

What is the Jubilee Sabbath Year? The Bible describes a period of time most people have never heard of. It occurs after seven sets of seven yearly intervals (Seven Shemitah Cycles) are finished. This proclamation of a fiftieth "liberty" year occurs on one of God's annual feasts days on the Day of Atonement. God set up a special, regularly *set time* period where Jubilee is not just for allowing the land to rest. It is a reminder, just like the weekly Sabbath, that God has created everything. It is also a reminder that we are not the only owners of the land.

The Jubilee Sabbath Year started on Yom Kippur on September 23, 2015, and concludes October 12, 2016, before America's presidential election. America will conclude Columbus Day at the same time the Jubilee Sabbath Year ends. Isn't this fascinating that the Jubilee of Israel coincides with America's day of discovery by a Messianic Jew? Just a coincidence you say? Is this yet another example of our spiritual connection to Israel?

One cannot help but to be intrigued by the unique and very rare occurrence of the Four Blood Moon Tetrad of 2014-15 and the fact that it occurred during a Shemitah Sabbath Year. Now the Jubilee Sabbath Year follows with another set of unique features. Isn't it exciting we're the generation that's been selected by God for this *set time*? What is it going to bring to America?

This fiftieth year is sacred. It is a time of freedom and celebration, once in a generation when everyone in ancient Israel would receive back their original deeded property, and slaves would return home to their families. During a Jubilee Sabbath Year, a nation that honors and obeys God will be blessed and would

94

receive a tremendous blessing if they observed this part of God's law. However, a nation that rejects God and His law could face God's judgment and wrath.

Josephus the Jewish historian, in his monumental work on the history of the Jewish people, discusses historical events that he felt occurred during Jubilee years such as *Antiochus'* besieging of Jerusalem. In *Herod the Great's* thirteenth year of rule there was famine and corresponding pestilence, the worst since the time of *King Ahab*. Josephus states it occurred in a Jubilee year.

There are many fine biblical researchers and ministers who differ on correctly calculating the Jubilee Sabbath Year, so I won't go into all the detail. But, 2015-16, not 2017 is the Jubilee Sabbath Year. How is it calculated? There are two basic things to remember when calculating the Jubilee;

1. After seven Shemitah Cycles (every 7th year of release; 7 x 7 = 49 years) have been observed, the next year, the 50th is the Jubilee Sabbath Year. It is also the first year of a next Shemitah and new Jubilee Cycle. The word Jubilee itself has a Gematria value of 53, which we will discuss in more detail later in this text.

2. The Jubilee Sabbath Year begins and ends in the fall.

Many calculate the Jubilee this way: because 1917 was the year of the Balfour Declaration and because in 1967 was the year Jerusalem was returned as the capital of Israel, many make the following miscalculation to find the next Jubilee year: 1917+50=1967+50=2017. The proper way to calculate the next Jubilee Sabbath Year is as follows:

Fall 1917-Fall 1918+49 years = Fall 1966-Fall 1967+49 years = Fall 2015-Fall 2016.

This is also the only method in which the Balfour Declaration (November 2, 1917) and the capture of the Old City of Jerusalem (June 7, 1967) can fall within the actual Jubilee Sabbath

Year. Incorrectly adding 50 years to November/December 1917 puts the Jubilee beginning in the fall of 1967, which means that the recapture of Jerusalem in June 1967 occurs before the Jubilee begins. If you go back 50 years from June 1967, instead of 49, then the Balfour Declaration occurs after the Jubilee ends in fall 1917.

Furthermore, Rabbi Jonathan Cahn has laid out the Shemitah Sabbath Years to the exact day, and those cycles are 2000-2001, 2007-2008, and 2014-2015. The Jubilee of 2015-2016 arrived in perfect succession. The puzzle pieces fit too perfectly to be a coincidence. So, with that out of the way, let's proceed.

The Jubilee does not begin on the New Year, but it begins 10 ten days later during the Day of Atonement. There is an extremely important reason for this. The Day of Atonement is when all of Israel's iniquities, transgressions, and sins were forgiven. However, it was not until the Day of Atonement had finished that they were clean before God and freed from the penalty of their sin. They had all day to realize that it took the sacrifice of shedding innocent blood in God's presence for their sins to be forgiven.

The Jubilee would come every 50 years, and it would put an end to financial oppression. In ancient Israel, slaves were set free, and mortgages ended. All bondage was broken, and the people would be free to start fresh. It was also a year of agricultural rest as there would be no farming during this year. God promised to bless the crops and orchards abundantly, and the people were to rest from their labor. It was a year to focus on God and not farming, money, or social problems. It was a time of restoration.

The object of the year of Jubilee was to obtain liberty and to break all oppression. The Jubilee was a type or forerunner of what it would be under the reign of Jesus Christ. The Jubilee was to set the stage for the coming of Jesus as His reign would be one continual Jubilee. All oppression would end under His rule. Justice and truth would reign. All financial bondage would end. There would be peace and an abundance of crops. There will be real freedom from captivity, confinement, or physical restraint under the rule of Jesus.

The Jubilee year is the year at the end of seven cycles of Shemitah, and according to Biblical regulations had a special impact on the ownership and management (leadership) of the land; Jubilee deals largely with land, property, and property rights. The biblical rules concerning Sabbatical years are still observed by many religious Jews in Israel. According to Leviticus, slaves and prisoners would be freed, debts would be forgiven, and the mercies of God would be particularly manifested.

The Septuagint rendered the Hebrew *yovel* as *"a trumpet-blast of liberty."* Traditionally, it was thought that the English term Jubilee derives from the Hebrew term *yobel.* That word, in turn, derives from *yobhel,* meaning ram; the Jubilee year was announced by a *"Trump"* on a shofar, an instrument made from a ram's horn, during that year's Yom Kippur.

Leviticus 25:8-13 states; *"You shall count off seven Sabbaths of years, seven times seven years; and there shall be to you the days of seven Sabbaths of years, even forty-nine years. Then you shall sound the loud trumpet on the tenth day of the seventh month. On the Day of Atonement you shall sound the trumpet throughout all your land. You shall make the fiftieth year holy, and proclaim liberty throughout the land to all its inhabitants. It shall be a Jubilee to you; and each of you shall return to his own property, and each of you shall return to his family. That fiftieth year shall be a Jubilee to you. In it you shall not sow, neither reap that which grows of itself, nor gather from the undressed vines. For it is a Jubilee; it shall be holy to you. You shall eat of its increase out of the field. In this Year of Jubilee each of you shall return to his property."*

As the Jewish New Year began on September 13, 2015, on the Jewish Feast of Trumpets of Rosh Hashanah, a Partial Solar Eclipse took place. Jewish Rabbis consider a solar eclipse to mean a harsh period, of time or a "bad omen" for Gentile countries of the world. Since the eclipse, terror attacks have intensified worldwide by radical jihadists as they try to form an *Islamic Caliphate* to bring forth their messiah, the *Twelfth Imam, the Mahdi.*

Storm clouds again are indeed gathering over God's chosen people for the Gospel of Yeshua. *ISIS* terror army has conquered huge areas of Syria and Iraq. Iran struck a landmark nuclear deal with the rest of the world, Russia made its biggest military move in decades into the Middle East. The country of Turkey exhibited a failed military coup of its national leadership.

These series of converging events will create a situation far more dangerous in the near future. We may be watching a prophetic sign that applies to everyone. Sitting right in the center of the middle of the storm is the nation of Israel and the City of Jerusalem. The tiny nation of Israel stands squarely in the crosshairs of evil and determined enemies who want nothing more than to push them into the sea. Surrounded by enemies in a volatile region, we see more than ever the growing importance for America to stand with Israel.

"Be strong and be of good courage, fear not, nor be afraid of them: for the LORD thy God, he it is that doth go with thee, he will not fail thee, nor forsake thee."
Deuteronomy 31:6

America's leaders continue openly to defile and mock God; they seek to isolate and partition Israel. It has intensified more rapidly as the current Obama Administration's tenure comes to an end with the promotion of gay marriage, transgender bathrooms, and abortion. Pure evil is continually celebrated by liberals on the left as 3,000 abortions are performed daily in America. The wholesale slaughter of our unborn children for the retail sale of their parts for profit disgusts me. The Democratic Presidential Nominee, Hillary Clinton in a recent debate said that she would continue this practice if elected.

Like we learned previously in Rabbi Cahn's book <u>The Harbinger</u>, God lifted His hedge of protection from Israel when they turned away from Him and the covenant. Israel's enemies, the terrorists, were allowed to defeat them in the Old Testament. If we as a nation don't turn back to God, evil will indeed overtake the United States, and God will judge America like He did ancient Israel. The five scariest words in the Bible are, *"...and God gave them over."*

AMERICA'S CONNECTION TO JUBILEE

"And ye shall hallow the fiftieth year, and proclaim liberty throughout the land unto all the inhabitants thereof; it shall be a Jubilee unto you; and ye shall return every man unto his possession, and ye shall return every man unto his family."
Leviticus 25:10

It is one of America's most famous relics, a nearly sacred totem. Several million people each year make a pilgrimage to see it, many dabbing their eyes as they gaze at it intently. Around the world, it is regarded as a universal symbol of freedom. The *Liberty Bell* is an iconic symbol of American independence, located in Philadelphia, Pennsylvania. The Liberty Bell was commissioned from the London firm of *Lester and Pack* in 1752 and was cast with the *lettering "Proclaim LIBERTY throughout all the land unto all the inhabitants thereof."*

The bell first cracked when rung after its arrival in Philadelphia and was twice recast by local workmen *John Pass and John Stow*, whose last names appear on the bell. It was used by our founding fathers to sound calls for the General Assembly of the legislature and to alert citizens to public meetings and proclamations. Like a *shofar trump-blast* was used in ancient Israel to summon gatherings. Wait a minute! The Liberty Bell is also connected to both Jubilee and Israel? Is this yet again a solid example of the spiritual connection between Israel and the United States? Check it out for yourself!

The bell's first inscribed line quotes part of the verse found in the King James Bible version of Leviticus 25:10 which mentions the Jubilee. The bell rang on July 8, 1776, to summon the people to hear the *Declaration of Independence*. Formerly placed in the steeple of the Pennsylvania State House (now renamed Independence Hall), the bell is located today in the Liberty Bell Center of Independence National Historical Park.

The city, in which the bell sets, Philadelphia, was founded, developed, and named "brotherly love" by William Penn in 1682. A man of extreme religious convictions, Penn wrote numerous works in which he exhorted believers to adhere to the spirit of Christianity. He was imprisoned several times in the *Tower of London* due to his faith. His book, <u>No Cross, No Crown</u> (1669), was written while in prison. Penn was an English, real estate entrepreneur, philosopher, early Quaker, and founder of the Province of Pennsylvania. He was an early advocate of democracy and religious freedom, notable for his good relations and successful treaties with Native Americans.

Philadelphia was also instrumental in the American Revolution as a meeting place for our Founding Fathers who signed the Declaration of Independence in 1776 and the Constitution in 1787. Philadelphia was one of the nation's capitals in the Revolutionary War served as temporary capital while Washington, D.C. was under construction. God intended from the beginning the city's very foundation to *"proclaim liberty throughout all the land"* making the city and the Liberty Bell well suited for each other.

Speaker of the Pennsylvania Assembly, *Isaac Norris*, chose this inscription for the State House bell in 1751, possibly to commemorate the 50th anniversary of *William Penn's 1701 Charter of Privileges*, which *granted religious liberties* and political self-government to the people of Pennsylvania.

The State House bell became a herald of liberty in the 19th century. *"Proclaim Liberty throughout all the land unto all the inhabitants thereof,"* the bell's inscription, provided a rallying cry for abolitionists wishing to end slavery. The Anti-Slavery Record, an abolitionist publication, first referred to the bell as the Liberty Bell in 1835, but that name was not widely adopted until years later.

The Liberty Bell has indeed captured Americans' affections and become a stand-in for the nation's vaunted values: independence, freedom, religious liberties, unalienable rights, and equality. It is virtually a touchstone of American identity because Americans have adopted it, along with the flag, as the symbol of justice, the rule of law, and the guardian of sovereign rights. America grew from thirteen colonies to fifty states. These fifty states are united to embolden life, liberty, and the pursuit of happiness.

On the 50th anniversary of the signing of the *Declaration of Independence*, July 4, 1826, two former presidents, *Thomas Jefferson* and *John Adams*, who were once fellow *Patriots*, died on the same day. Although their opinions on governmental power differed for many years, they had both believed in democracy and life, liberty and the pursuit of happiness. Thomas Jefferson and John Adams were the last surviving members of the original American revolutionaries who had stood up to the *British Empire* and forged a new political system. They renewed their friendship in their golden years and died within five hours of each other.

This is also very interesting, possibly means nothing, but still is fascinating with both the numbers 50 and 13; the backbone of America, United States Route 50 (US 50), is a major east–west route of the highway system, stretching just over 3,000 miles, "coast to coast" from the Atlantic to the Pacific. From Sacramento, California to Ocean City, Maryland on the Atlantic Ocean, US 50 passes through a total of 13 providences with the District of Columbia, California, Nevada, Utah, Colorado, Kansas, Missouri, Illinois, Indiana, Ohio, West Virginia, Virginia, and Maryland.

An interesting connection America has with Israel, and this one deals with music. A melody written originally about Jerusalem became one of our most favorite. Remember the patriotic song *"America the Beautiful?"* "America! America! God shed His grace on thee, and crown thy good with brotherhood, from sea to shining sea!" Did you sing it in grade school? Returning in 1893 from an inspiring trip to Pikes Peak in Colorado, *Katherine Lee Bates* wrote a poem/prayer she titled "America." It was printed the following year in a church publication in Boston to commemorate the Fourth of July.

Samuel A. Ward church organist and choirmaster composed the music. He had originally written the music, *"Materna"* for the hymn *"O Mother Dear, Jerusalem"* in 1882. Ward's music combined with the Bates' poem was first published in 1910. It quickly caught the public's fancy. Just think about how cool this really is; a melody by Samuel A. Ward about Jerusalem and a prayer for America by Katharine Lee Bates, is still one of the most popular American patriotic songs still to this day. American children have been singing a prayer and blessing set to a melody about Jerusalem all these years, and they didn't even know it!

At various times in the more than 100 years since the song was written, there have been efforts to give "America the Beautiful" legal status either as a national hymn or as a national anthem equal to, or in place of, *"The Star-Spangled Banner."* Generations have sung this song about America that we learned as children. It is a beautiful expression of what our great country means to us.

However, did you know this song is also connected to Jubilee? The last verse of the original poem was changed in 1904 to the version we now know. But in the original poem, the last verse reads, "God shed his grace on thee, Till nobler men keep once again, Thy *Whiter Jubilee!*" Whiter Jubilee is a reference to scripture found in the Bible. Revelation 3:4-5 describes those who are moral and just as deserving of wearing white; and then goes on to describe the throne room of heaven as populated by the great multitude wearing white in Revelation 7:9-17. Bates was asking with her original poem, that God protect America until men are noble enough to celebrate God's yet *Whiter Jubilee* with the return of Jesus Christ! Yeshua!

RELIGIOUS FREEDOM AND LIBERTIES

American pastors have historically addressed politics from the pulpit, offering biblical context to the controversial political issues of the day. In fact, churches often served as a catalyst for change in America, playing a dominant role in the abolition of slavery.

For almost the first 200 years in America, pastors spoke freely and boldly from their pulpit about the issues of the day. It was also not uncommon for pastors to publicly oppose candidates they saw unfit for political office. There is a long history of American pastors preaching election sermons, bringing biblical truth to bear on the citizenship responsibility of Americans in selecting government leaders.

"The church must take right ground in regard to politics. Politics are a part of a religion in such a country as this, and Christians must do their duty to the country as part of their duty to God. God will bless or curse this nation according to the course Christians take in politics."

Rev. Charles G. Finney, 1835

However, in 1954, the passage of one piece of legislation effectively overturned this freedom. This was the *Johnson Amendment*. Today, the Internal Revenue Service (IRS) can use the Johnson Amendment to tell pastors what they can and cannot preach. This is the government's attempt to weaken the influence of evangelicals as a political voting alliance in America. This limits their protection under the *First Amendment* for Free Speech and limits religious liberties and freedom. This law aims to censor sermons if the IRS labels it "political." This was not the intent of our founding fathers and is clearly a violation of free speech.

The Johnson Amendment refers to a change in the United States tax code made in 1954. It prohibited certain tax-exempt organizations from endorsing and opposing political candidates.

Proposed by then-Senator Lyndon B. Johnson of Texas, the same who later would become president and later choose not to support Israel and run for reelection in 1968.

The amendment affects churches and other nonprofit organizations with 501(c) (3) tax exemptions. 501(c) prohibition: Organizations recognized under Section 501(c) (3) of the United States tax code is subject to limits or absolute prohibitions on engaging in political activities and risk loss of tax exempt status if violated. Specifically, they are prohibited from conducting political campaign activities to intervene in elections to public office.

The Internal Revenue Service website elaborates upon this prohibition as follows:

Under the Internal Revenue Code, all section 501(c)(3) organizations are absolutely prohibited from directly or indirectly participating in, or intervening in, any political campaign on behalf of (or in opposition to) any candidate for elective public office. Contributions to political campaign funds or public statements of position (verbal or written) made on behalf of the organization in favor of or in opposition to any candidate for public office, clearly violate the prohibition against political campaign activity. Violating this prohibition may result in denial or revocation of tax-exempt status and the imposition of certain excise taxes.

Certain activities or expenditures may not be prohibited depending on the facts and circumstances. For example, certain voter education activities, including presenting public forums and publishing voter education guides, conducted in a non-partisan manner, do not constitute prohibited political campaign activity. In addition, other activities intended to encourage people to participate in the electoral process, such as voter registration and get-out-the-vote drives, would not be prohibited political campaign activity if conducted in a non-partisan manner.

On the other hand, voter education or registration activities with evidence of bias that (a) would favor one candidate over another; (b) oppose a candidate in some manner, or (c) have the effect of favoring a candidate or group of candidates, will constitute prohibited participation or intervention.

The Internal Revenue Service provides resources to exempt organizations and the public to help them understand the prohibition. As part of its examination program, the IRS also monitors whether organizations are complying with the prohibition.

If you've been paying any attention to politics and watching the Republican Presidential Nominee Donald Trump closely, you've heard him mention the "Johnson Amendment." Trump said, "We call it the Johnson Amendment, where you are just absolutely shunned if you're evangelical. If you want to talk religion, you lose your tax-exempt status."

At the Republican National Convention during his acceptance speech, Donald Trump said, "At this moment, I would like to thank the evangelical and religious community in general who have been so good to me and so supportive. You have much to contribute to our politics, yet our laws prevent you from speaking your minds from your own pulpits."

"An amendment, pushed by Lyndon Johnson, many years ago, threatens religious institutions with a loss of their tax-exempt status if they openly advocate their political views. I am going to work very hard to repeal that language and protect free speech for all Americans."

The new Republican Party platform references the policy: Republicans believe the federal government, specifically the IRS, is constitutionally prohibited from policing or censoring speech based on religious convictions or beliefs, and therefore we urge the repeal of the Johnson Amendment.

Under current federal tax law, tax-exempt churches of worship are not allowed to intervene in partisan political campaigns. Ministries can obviously speak out on moral and spiritual issues of the day, but churches and other houses of worship can't when it involves politics. The First Amendment's protection of free-speech, as far as the argument goes, should also apply to pastors in the pulpit. They should be able to say whatever they wish to their congregation, and it's not the government's job to intervene.

As for the First Amendment, tax-exempt entities, including churches, have the option of getting engaged in partisan politics, endorsing candidates, and intervening in campaigns to their hearts' content, but they can't do this while keeping their tax exemption.

Trump is saying he wants to scrap the Johnson Amendment when elected; churches should have *religious liberties* and get the benefit of a tax exemption from the government, without any of the conditions like in the past. *"Proclaim Liberty throughout all the land unto all the inhabitants thereof."*

THE GREGORIAN AND HEBREW CALENDAR

The *Gregorian Calendar,* also called the *Western Calendar,* or the *Christian Calendar*, is internationally the most widely used. The Gregorian calendar is a solar calendar year which consists of 365.25 days. In a leap year (every four years), a leap day is added, and February 29th is often considered as the leap day.

Okay, are you confused? We're about to go somewhere! I want to show you that the Hebrew Calendar in the Bible is different from our Western Calendar. Jewish feasts and holidays for centuries have all started and ended with the Hebrew lunar calendar. God has shown us that certain dates and patterns repeat themselves (*set time*). So it's best that we understand the difference between the two calendars.

The *Hebrew Calendar* is a lunisolar calendar, meaning that months are based on lunar months. The calendar year features twelve lunar months of 29 or 30 days, with an *intercalary*. Intercalary is the insertion of a leap day, week, or month into some calendar years to make the calendar follow the seasons or moon phases. A lunar month is added periodically every two to three years (Adar II) to synchronize the twelve lunar cycles with the longer solar year on the Hebrew Calendar.

Ever heard the term once in a *blue moon*? The phrase has nothing to do with the actual color of the moon; although, a literal "blue moon" (the moon appearing with a tinge of blue) may occur in certain atmospheric conditions. The term has traditionally referred to an "extra" full moon in one month, where a full year, which normally has twelve full moons, has thirteen instead. This happens every two to three years. Seven times in the previous 19-years there have been thirteen full moons in a year. The most recent blue moon was on May 21, 2016. The Maine Farmers' Almanac states the next blue moons will occur on January 31, 2018, and again on May 18, 2019.

The beginning of each Jewish lunar month is based on the reappearance of the *new moon* (the moon being reborn). Originally, the new lunar crescent had to be observed and certified by two witnesses. The Hebrew calendar year begins with the month of *Nisan*. Nisan is the first month of the ecclesiastical year and begins in the spring. In ancient Israel, the start of the ecclesiastical New Year for the counting of months and festivals was determined in reference to the Feast of Passover. Passover is on *14th of Nisan*, (Leviticus 23:4–6) which corresponds to the full moon of Nisan. Passover is a spring festival; it should fall on a full moon day, and normally just after the *equinox*.

The day most commonly referred to as the "New Year" is on the *1st of Tishrei*, which actually begins in the seventh month of the ecclesiastical year and begins the season for the fall feasts. The month of Tishrei starts the formal New Year for the counting of years (such as Shemitah and Jubilee); Rosh Hashanah (head of the year) is observed (See Ezekiel 40:1, which uses the phrase "beginning of the year").

Jonathan Cahn showed us in <u>the Harbinger</u> the pattern for the *29th of Elul*. At the end of a Shemitah Sabbath Year, the American stock market crashed seven years apart on the same day. God establishes cycles and patterns and once established, it doesn't change. If God started it, God is going to finish it. Dates are important in Hebrew history for remembrance just as dates in America have significance too, like December 7th and September 11th. I'm going to show you some prophetic dates for America coming in the near future on the Hebrew calendar and compare them to the Gregorian. Let's see if, the modern-day Sons of Issachar can discern a spiritual prophetic connection.

Tammuz is the fourth month of the ecclesiastical year on the Hebrew calendar. It is a summer month of 29 days, which occurs on the Gregorian calendar around June and July. One particular day, the *17th of Tammuz* starts with a period of mourning commemorating the destruction of the *First and Second Jewish Temples*. These periods start with the *Three Weeks Fast* and ends with the *Fast of Tisha B'Av*, on the *9th of Av*. Both of these fasts commemorate events surrounding the destruction of the Jewish Temples and the subsequent Jewish Exile from the land of Israel.

The Three Weeks are historically a time of misfortune since many tragedies and calamities befell the Jewish people at this time. These tragedies include, a time referred to as a day of sin when Israel offered up an idol, the *Golden Calf,* (referred to as "the day of sin") (Exodus 32:4).

The day Moses smashed the first two tablets of the Ten Commandments (the Law). Also occurred on the 17th of Tammuz was the day when daily sacrifices in the *First Temple* was discontinued in 586 BC during the Babylon Siege of Nebuchadnezzar, and the Walls of Jerusalem were breached by the Roman Tenth Legion in 70 AD leading to the destruction of the *Second Temple*.

Remember the 1956 Charlton Heston Movie, *"The Ten Commandments?"* In the movie, the Hebrews camp at the foot of *Mount Sinai* and wait as Moses again ascends the mountain with Joshua, and they remained there for forty days. During his absence, the Hebrew's lose faith and grow impatient when it seemed that Moses was not coming down when promised. Urged by Dathan, they build a *Golden Calf* as an idol to take back to Egypt, hoping to win Rameses' forgiveness. They force Aaron to help fashion the gold plating. The people indulge their most malicious desires in an orgy of sinfulness, except for a few still loyal to Moses, including Lilia, Joshua, Zipporah, and Bithiah.

On the 17th of Tammuz, *"the Day of Sin,"* high atop the mountain, Moses witnesses God's creation of the stone tablets containing the Ten Commandments. When Moses finally climbs down and meets Joshua, they both behold their people's iniquity. Moses hurls the tablets (the Law) at the idol in a rage, smashing the tablets into the idol. Moses tells Dathan and his followers to choose God or Egypt. They are separated and are killed by God as an Earthquake swallows them up.

In the movie, afterward, God forces the remaining Hebrews to endure forty years of exile in the desert to kill off the rebellious generation before they arrive in the *Land of Canaan*. An elderly Moses, who is not allowed to enter the *Promised Land* because of his disobedience to God at the *Waters of Strife,* appoints Joshua to succeed him as leader. After forty years of wandering in the desert, Moses died on *Mount Nebo* within sight of the Promised Land. He says a final goodbye to his wife Zipporah and goes forth to his destiny.

Well, the actual Exodus story is written a little differently than the movie, but I think you get the idea and picture in your mind what happened on that day in Tammuz. On the Gregorian calendar in 2016, Tammuz falls in July and August. The summer of 2016, as America got ready to watch the political conventions and the *Olympics*, the Holy Spirit told me to look at the calendar. I didn't understand it at the time, so it took me awhile. But when I did, I found something very interesting and very prophetic.

The Democratic National Convention (DNC), started the same weekend in Philadelphia on the *17th of Tammuz*. I find it noteworthy that the DNC was held in Philadelphia during a Jubilee Sabbath Year where both the Declaration of Independence and the Constitution were born, and the Liberty Bell sits, to *"proclaim liberty throughout the land unto all the inhabitants thereof."* Wait! Wasn't Pope Francis just there too in September 2015? What's going on in Philadelphia?

The Democrat Party removed God from their party platform and continues to undermine the Constitution (the Law). Much like ancient Israel did before their destruction? Is there a pattern? As I watched the DNC, a grieving sickness came up from my stomach, as bile-filled in my throat. I tried not to puke in my living room as I looked over the delegates. I couldn't help but be reminded of the 1956 Charlton Heston Movie, "The Ten Commandments."

Like the lawless and corrupt slaves of Egypt in the movie, I saw in the DNC a picture of the same obscene and perverted spirit. It appeared to me that the DNC had been possessed by foul spirits and hell's demons. I saw God defiled, booed, and mocked with filth and vulgarity as rainbow flags of LGBT were prevalent. Transgender-confusion and abortions were cheered like a Democrat badge of honor to those on the political left.

"Be not deceived, God is not mocked: for whatsoever a man soweth, that shall he also reap."

Galatians 6:7

I saw no American flags on stage the first day, but saw Palestinian flags being waived by delegates on television while both flags of the United States and Israel were burned outside by protestors all in the name of "Free-Speech." As a Christian affectionate to both Israel and America, I grieved deep in my heart.

John the Baptist preaching in the wilderness about Jesus said in Matthew 3:12, *"Whose fan is in his hand, and he will thoroughly purge his floor, and gather his wheat into the garner; but he will burn up the chaff with unquenchable fire."*

Jesus said in Matthew 25:31-46, *"The Son of Man will judge the nations gathered before Him. He will set the sheep on His right hand but the goats on the left. Then He will also say to those on the left, depart from Me, you cursed, into the everlasting fire prepared for the devil and his angels."*

"And I will bless them that bless thee, and curse him that curseth thee: and in thee shall all families of the earth be blessed."

Genesis 12:3

I find it very prophetic that the DNC decided to hold their convention in the very city founded on religious liberty, where the Liberty Bell is on display, the city where our Founding Fathers conceived a Nation Under God, signed the Declaration of Independence, and Constitution for our republic guaranteeing our inevitable rights and religious freedom. The DNC platform seems to be just the opposite. They aren't lovers of the truth; they're lovers of themselves! However, I am reminded again of the 1956 Charlton Heston movie of what God did to those lawless and corrupt Children of Israel on Mount Sinai as they chose a golden idol over God.

"This know also, that in the last days perilous times shall come. For men shall be lovers of their own selves, covetous, boasters, proud, blasphemers, disobedient to parents, unthankful, unholy. Without natural affection, trucebreakers, false accusers, incontinent, fierce, despisers of those that are good, Traitors, heady, high minded, lovers of pleasures more than lovers of God; Having a form of godliness, but denying the power thereof: from such turn away. For of this sort are they which creep into houses, and lead captive silly women laden with sins, led away with divers lusts, Ever learning, and never able to come to the knowledge of the truth."

2 Timothy 3: 1-7

"Knowing this first, that there shall come in the last days scoffers, walking after their own lusts, and saying, where is the promise of his coming? For since the fathers fell asleep, all things continue as they were from the beginning of the creation."

2 Peter 3:3-4

The month of *Cheshvan* is the eighth month of the ecclesiastical year on the Hebrew calendar. It is an autumn month of 29 -30 days, which occurs on the Gregorian calendar around October and November. Praying for rain is the essence of the Land of Israel. Cheshvan, (sometimes called Marcheshvan) in Hebrew, is *"Mar,"* and means "Drop of Water." This is when the rain begins.

Jewish Rabbis declare that the spirituality experienced in the previous month of Tishrei, during the fall feasts, doesn't just end abruptly. They cite the principle that a Jew must always ascend in holiness. One must constantly be climbing higher and higher in the service to God. Jews are taught that Cheshvan is "reserved" for the time of *Moshiach* (mah-SHEE-ahkh), the anointed one. The word is generally translated as "messiah," but the Jewish concept is very different from the Christian one; He will be a man who will be chosen by God to put an end to all evil in the world connecting with anointed Godliness. He will rebuild the *Third Temple*; bring the exiles back to Israel, and usher in the world to come.

Jewish tradition says *Methuselah* dies at the age of 969 (Genesis 5:27), and it began to rain shortly thereafter. The *Great Flood* in the days of Noah began during the month of Cheshvan. It was a year later, in the same month of Cheshvan, when Noah left the Ark (Genesis 8:14). Moreover, Cheshvan is the only month in the Jewish calendar which does not have a holiday, making it a unique month.

There is one apparently minor event associated with Cheshvan which gives a clue regarding what is expected during that month. Likewise, this is indeed an expression of "ascending in holiness." During the *Second Temple Era* (circa 230 BC), the 7th of *Cheshvan* was the date on which the Jews that lived most distant from the Holy Temple arrived back home from their pilgrimage.

Some resided on the banks of the *Euphrates River*, as it took a 15-day journey from Jerusalem upon returning from their Sukkot pilgrimage (Feast of Tabernacles). Historically, all Jews would wait for this day before beginning to pray for rain on the 7th of *Cheshvan*. It was; therefore, appropriate to begin praying for rain from this point on, but not before. Therefore, Jews in Israel begin to pray for rain in their daily prayer on this day for harvest.

The rain begins in the fall season in Israel as the Jews begin to pray for rain for both their physical and spiritual harvest. The physical seeds that were planted in the soil and the spiritual pilgrimage in the month of Tishrei both must now be watered and carefully nurtured in order to harvest. Jews believe with God's help; a bumper spiritual crop will bring out the very best in them, through their own hard work, and thus transform bitterness into sweetness.

"For I will pour water upon him that is thirsty, and floods upon the dry ground: I will pour my spirit upon thy seed, and my blessing upon thine offspring."

Isaiah 44:3

So again I felt the Holy Spirit telling me to look at the calendar. This time I was obedient much quicker. So you may begin to ask yourself, what is the *7th of Cheshvan* in 2016 on the Gregorian Calendar? Could this be a prophetic message to America concerning the presidential election? The *7th of Cheshvan* in 2016 is Tuesday, November 8th. America's Election Day! The day it begins to rain! I'm sure you'll get it in a minute!

THE SIGNIFICANCE OF NUMBERS

Let me begin by saying that I think we need to be careful about hidden messages, meanings, or codes with certain significant numbers in the Bible. If you put the word *"Numerology"* in a Google search, what you get is a definition: "The branch of knowledge that deals with the occult significance of numbers." Hence, "Numerology" is associated with such things as the occult, the paranormal, astrology, paganism, divination, and Wiccans. If we put "Biblical" in front of "Numerology" ("Biblical Numerology"), then maybe searching for the significance of number meanings in the Bible is more acceptable. God most definitely has order and patterns; we need to be aware of them and pay attention to the Sons of Issachar.

I am not saying that there isn't some significance to certain numbers in the Bible. We all are familiar with numbers in the Bible. All I am saying is that we should be careful to interpret what these meanings are. I believe God did have reasons for using certain numbers over and over in the Bible, but only He knows the true reason. Having said this, I do think it is fascinating to see how many times certain key numbers are repeatedly used in the Bible.

God's works are perfect, and His words are perfect. Can there also be perfection in His use of numbers? The Jews and early Christians of the Old and New Testaments thought so, and so did the Fathers of the Catholic Church. *Saint Jerome, Saint Augustine, and Pope Saint Gregory I,* all wrote extensively of God's design and the significance of His plan of salvation in the use of numbers. So did *Leonardo da Vinci* and *Sir Isaac Newton.* According to ancient tradition, each number has significance, and each Hebrew letter has a numerical value. Ancient Mystic-Jews also believed that the Word of God held hidden meaning. They used a system called Gematria to unlock them.

What is Gematria? It is a Jewish system of numerology that assigns numeral values to words, names, and phrases. Each of the 22 letters of the Hebrew alphabet corresponds to a number. For example, the first letter of the Hebrew alphabet is *aleph* with a numerical value of 1. The second letter of the alphabet is *bet* with a numerical value of 2, and so on, ending the alphabet with the letter *Tav* which has a numerical value of 400. Do we see Gematria in the Bible? The answer is yes! Gematria is Biblical. In Revelation 13:18, *"Here is wisdom. Let him that hath understanding count the number of the beast: for it is the number of man; and his number is six hundred threescore and six (666)."*

In the original Hebrew version of the Bible, in the Book of Daniel 8:13, there is a *"Saint"* called *Palmoni*. The King James Version refers to *Palmoni* indirectly as *"that certain saint."* Strong's Concordance uses a margin note from oral traditions that translates it as, *"The numberer of secrets."* Palmoni literally means *"Wonderful Numberer."* This Wonderful Numberer is none other than the LORD Jesus Christ (read Isaiah 9:6). Only Jesus Christ Himself, He alone, the Master of all numbers, can count the stars in heaven and the hairs on your head.

"Who has measured the waters in the hollow of His hand; and meted out heaven with a span; and comprehended the dust of the earth in a measure, and weighed the mountains in scales, and the hills in a balance?"

Isaiah 40:12

"Teach us to number our days aright, that we may gain wisdom of heart."

Psalm 90:12

These are the key numbers in the Bible that I find are frequently used: 3, 6, 7, 8, 10, 12, 40, 50, 70, and 120. But let's take a brief look below at two numbers that relate to this manuscript and what God has shown me personally.

The Number 3: What is the significance of the number 3 in the Bible? *"Holy, Holy, Holy"* is the LORD God Almighty (Isaiah 6:3 and Revelation 4:8).

Three is the number of perfect completion for the Jews, though to a lesser degree than the number 7. For Christians, the number 3 symbolizes the perfection of unity; the Holy Trinity of the Father, Son, and Holy Spirit; Faith, Hope, and Love; Past, Present, and Future; Yesterday, Today, and Tomorrow.

In the Book of Genesis, the word God is used 33 times. In the very beginning of the Book of Revelation, the number 3 is as a Being *"which is, and which was, and which is to come."*

Revelation 1:4

The number 3 is used 467 times in the Bible. The 3 righteous patriarchs before the flood were Abel, Enoch, and Noah: after the deluge, there were the righteous fathers Abraham, Isaac and, Jacob (later renamed Israel). There are only 3 angels named in the Bible: Michael, Gabriel, and Lucifer.

There are 27 books in the New Testament, which is 3 x 3 x 3, or completeness to the third power.

Appearances of the number 3: There were only three individuals who witnessed Jesus' appearance on the *Mount of Transfiguration*. Those who saw Jesus' glory on the mount were John, Peter, and James (see Matthew 17:1-8).

Jesus prayed three times in the Garden of Gethsemane before His arrest (Matthew 26:36-46, Mark 14:32-42). Jesus performed 33 miracles. Jesus was about 33 when he died. Mark 15:25 tells us that Jesus was placed on the cross at the 3rd hour of the day (9 a.m.) and died at the 9th hour (3 p.m.) There were 3 hours of darkness (eclipse) that covered the land while Jesus was suffering on the cross from the 6th hour to the 9th hour (Mark 15:33-34). Jesus was dead for 3 full days and 3 full nights, before being resurrected on the first day of the week (John 20:1).

This number is repeated throughout the Bible as a symbol of completeness. I could go on with more examples of the number 3 in Bible, but I think you get an idea of its importance.

The Number 50: Fifty is the number of Jubilee or deliverance of the Holy Spirit. Fifty can be found 154 times in the Bible. Its meaning is directly related to the coming of God's Holy Spirit. Of the five longest books in God's word, the Book of Genesis has 50 chapters. God promised Abraham that if he found only 50 righteous people in *Sodom* and *Gomorrah*, he would not destroy both cities (see Genesis 18:23 – 26).

On the 50th day after leaving Egypt, God met Israel at Mount Sinai; this was the first Pentecost (Exodus 19:1; 14-16). David bought the "threshing floor" located on Mount Moriah from Araunah the Jebusite for 50 shekels of silver in order to build an altar in this spot. Solomon later built the *First Temple* on this same site (see 2 Samuel 24:24).

In the New Testament, the word Pentecost comes from the Greek word for 50th, also known as the Feast of Weeks. After the seven weeks of harvest, the next day, the 50th day, is Pentecost. This day is also the first day of the week or the 8th day of the seventh week. It was on this special day that God first poured His Holy Spirit upon about 120 believers and disciples, who had gathered on *Mount Zion* in the *Upper Room* to keep the day. They became the First-Fruits of God's spiritual harvest (see Acts 1:15, 2-1).

In the 50th year, known as a Jubilee year, all debts were to be forgiven, all Hebrew slaves were to be freed, and all land was to be returned to the original owner. (Leviticus 25:8-19). Once again we can see God's pattern, particularly for the number 50 and its importance to His out pouring of the Holy Spirit. With that out of the way, we will be using this section for later examination when we explore the Jubilee patterns later in this text.

But first, let's put some of this together using previous sections on the Gregorian and Hebrew Calendars along with this section.

Jewish Rabbis believe there's prophetic meaning in numbers, and God has something special in each New Hebrew year to reveal. We will do the same, explore the numbers together, and find if there is any meaning to them. Let's look at the *Hebrew Year 5777*.

October 3, 2016, through September 20, 2017, on the Gregorian Calendar will be the Year 5777 on the Hebrew Calendar. It will begin on the Hebrew Calendar with, the *1ˢᵗ of Tishrei*, the beginning of the Jewish New Year at *Rosh Hashanah*. It will end on the *29ᵗʰ of Elul*.

The Biblical name for this holiday is *Yom Teruah*, meaning "day of shouting/blasting." It is sometimes known as the *Feast of Trumpets*. It is the only feast that starts with the sliver of a *new moon* and a trumpet-blast.

Rosh Hashanah is a 72 hour (3-day) celebration (no man knoweth the hour), which begins on the 1ˢᵗ day of Tishrei. Tishrei is the first month of the Jewish civil year, but the seventh month of the ecclesiastical year.

According to Judaism, written in the Talmud, the fact that Rosh Hashanah is the beginning of the year is explained by it being the traditional anniversary of the creation of Adam and Eve, the first man and woman. Rosh Hashanah customs include sounding the *"shofar"* (a hollowed-trump out ram's horn), as prescribed in the Torah, and following the inscription in the Hebrew Bible to "raise a noise" on Yom Teruah; and among its rabbinical customs, the common Hebrew greeting on Rosh Hashanah is *Shanah Tovah,* "have a happy year." Another is the eating of symbolic foods such as apples dipped in honey to evoke a "sweet new year."

If we pay attention and look at the numbers and their meaning, maybe there is, in fact, something we can conclude prophetically on what God has in store for us in the near future. Rabbis break down the symbols and letters as to their meanings.

Before we break down the meaning of the Hebrew Year 5777, let's quickly look back at World History to see if something leaps out.

First, October 31, 2017, will be the 500th year anniversary of the Protestant Reformation (10 Jubilees). The Protestant Reformation was the 16th-century religious, political, intellectual and cultural upheaval that splintered Catholic Europe, setting in place the structures and beliefs that would define the continent in the modern era.

In northern and central Europe, reformers like Martin Luther, John Calvin, and Henry VIII challenged papal authority and questioned the Catholic Church's ability to define Christian practice. They argued for religious liberty and political redistribution of power into the hands of pastors and princes. Can this be prophetic that *"religious liberty"* is also under attack in 5777 in a Jubilee Sabbath Year? Will there be a reformation in the Church in America?

Second, it will be the 100th year anniversary of the *Balfour Declaration* (2 Jubilees) on November 2, 2017. The agreed version of the declaration contained just 67 words.

Third, it will be the 50th year anniversary of the unification of the City of Jerusalem in Israel with the victory of the *Six-Day War* (1 Jubilee) on June 7, 2017.

All of these anniversaries are very important to both Christians and Jews. Because they are noteworthy, I want to point out the number significance of 50 within these anniversaries. It's here I want to remind you to not miss observing on August 21, 2017, the "Great American Total Solar Eclipse" where all 50 States of America will see in the Hebrew Year 5777.

Now let's look back at only Bible history and examine *Lamech*. Why Lamech? In the Bible, Lamech lived to be 777 years old, and it's the year 5777. Maybe we can find something prophetic by examining Lamech and his generation?

"The thing that hath been, it is that which shall be; and that which is done is that which shall be done: and there is no new thing under the sun."

Ecclesiastes 1:9

Lamech was the eighth descendant from Adam, (Genesis 5:25), the son of Methuselah and the father of Noah (Genesis 5:29). Let's look at the number eight briefly and discover any hidden meaning. The number eight in the Bible can signify a new beginning, a covenant sign, light, regeneration, resurrection, and the revival of a new era and order. The last of the seven feasts of Israel, the Feast of Tabernacles, lasts eight days. There were eight people in Noah's Ark.

The Festival of Lights (Hanukah) celebrates the Maccabee's triumph over the Greeks when the rededication of the temple and the relighting of the Menorah lasted eight days on a single day's supply of oil.

The resurrection of Jesus is the ultimate new beginning. Jesus entered Jerusalem on the 10th Day of Nisan as the lamb for his father's house (Read Exodus 12:3). He rode a colt, the foal of an ass. A crowd gathered and cut down branches and cast them in the way singing, *"HOSANNA; BLESSED IS HE THAT COMETH IN THE NAME OF THE LORD"*, and then He entered the temple (Mark 11:1-11). The crowd sang words of rejoice from Psalm 118:26 because they knew of the prophecy from Zechariah 9:9 where Zion's future king was to arrive in Jerusalem.

He was crucified on the 14th of Nisan (Passover) and placed in the tomb at the beginning of the Feast of Unleavened Bread before sunset. The Bible says Jesus rose on the first day (which is Sunday) of the next week (John 20:1) from the day He was

122

crucified. This was the beginning of the Feast of First Fruits (Leviticus 23:10-14). It was eight days from when He entered the city till His resurrection. Eight days is yet repeated again in Jesus's appearance to Thomas on the 8th day after his resurrection (see John 20:24).

Eight is the personal number of Jesus and the sign of the "new covenant" with Israel (Hebrews 8:8). Christ's title "Redeemer" occurs exactly eight times in the King James Version of the Bible. When we use Gematria in the Greek, we get 888 for the numerical value of the name of Jesus. The Greek system of numbering letters of the alphabet is called *Greek Isopsephy*. It predates and is based on a similar method to Hebrew Gematria.

In this system, each letter of the Greek alphabet is assigned a numerical value. The name of Jesus in Greek is spelled I H Σ O Y Σ (iota, eta, sigma, omicron, upsilon, and sigma). Substituting in the Greek numeral system the equivalent numerical values to each letter in the name of Jesus and adding them up, the total is **888**. This value is represented as Ω Π H (omega, pi, and eta).

I	iota	=	10
H	eta	=	8
Σ	sigma	=	200
O	omicron	=	70
Y	upsilon	=	400
Σ	sigma	=	200
Ω Π H	Total	=	888

In Hebrew Gematria, 888 amazingly show up as the sum total in several sentences and phrases in the Bible.

"The heavens declare the glory of God..."

Psalm 19:1

"...Our God forever and ever."

Psalm 48:14

"I am the Lord, I change not..."

Malachi 3:6

The Bible tells us after the resurrection of Jesus, he was seen by 512 people. Five hundred and twelve is the cube of the number eight (8x8x8).

"And that he was seen of Cephas, then of the twelve: After that, he was seen of above five hundred brethren at once; of whom the greater part remain unto this present, but some are fallen asleep."

1 Corinthians 15:5-6

Jesus calls himself the "Son of Man" as reference to the prophecy in Daniel 7:13-14. This term occurs 88 times in the King James Version of New Testament. Furthermore, "Jesus said" occurs in 65 exact phrases. "Said Jesus" occurs also in 23 exact phrases. Together in the King James Version of the New Testament, they add up to the following; 65 + 23 = 88.

We previous learned, there are 88 constellations in the heavens that declare the glory of God (see Psalm 19:1).

God commanded boys to be circumcised as the "Sign of the Covenant" to be performed on the 8th day (Genesis 17:12). *"And when eight days were accomplished for the circumcising of the child, his name was called JESUS, which was so named of the angel before he was conceived in the womb."*

Luke 2:21

In Luke 2:25-32, *"There was a man in Jerusalem called Simeon, who was righteous and devout, and the Holy Spirit was upon him. It had been revealed to him by the Holy Spirit that he would not die before he had seen the Lord's Christ. He went into the temple. When Joseph and Mary brought in the child Jesus to circumcise him what the custom of the Law required. Simeon took him in his*

124

arms and praised God, saying: 'Lord, as you have promised, you now dismiss your servant in peace. For my eyes have seen your salvation, which you have prepared in the sight of all people, a light for revelation to the Gentiles and for glory to your people Israel."

Wow! I must testify that it touches me in my spirit. Eight definitely has meaning; the sign of God's covenant and His Son Jesus. Did you learn anything?

Let's continue to review Lamech and his generation. Genesis 5:28-31 records that Lamech was 182 years old at the birth of Noah and lived for another 595 years, attaining an age at death of 777 years. With such numbers in this genealogical account, Adam would still have been alive for about the first 56 years of Lamech's life.

The Bible tells us that Adam (Genesis 5:5) lived 930 years which was long enough to see nine generations of offspring born from him. This would make Lamech Adam's great-great-great-great-great-great-grandson. Lamech was the sandwich generation between Methuselah his father and Noah, his son. Crazy to think about, but many generations of Adam could have literally worked on the Ark with Noah and his family. Can you imagine Grandfather Methuselah bouncing baby Shem on his knee and teaching him the redemption story in the stars?

Lamech means, *"Those in despair."* It can also mean strong youth, distressed, misery, desolation, destitute, hopelessness, anguish, gloom, depression, dependency, dejection, to lose hope, give up, lose heart, plumb to the depths, and see no light at the end. In Lamech's day, the generation of the world had become so corrupt and immoral. This was an evil time before the flood. Does this parallel the current situation and functioning of today's generation?

Lamech perceived a better future for coming generations as he uttered this prophecy, *"...This same shall comfort us concerning our work and toil of our hands, because of the ground which the LORD hath cursed."* (Genesis 5:29). This was a prediction of the coming flood and the restoration of the earth by Noah. However, how did Noah bring "comfort" against that vanity of life brought about by the curse put on sinful man?

The prophecy was fulfilled in that Noah authored a new creation by condemning the old one through his faith. He proved his faith by building the Ark (Hebrews 11:7-8). However, since Noah failed to remove the curse from the "new creation" (the curse continued into the New World even after the flood), we are made to look for a more complete fulfillment. Jesus Christ is that fulfillment. He is which leads us into a *"new creation"* (see 2 Corinthians 5:17).

When we look back at Lamech and his generation, could this be a clue to God's future plan for our current generation? God destroyed the corrupt and immoral with the flood but promised never to destroy the Earth again with water. We are reminded of His promise when we see a rainbow in the sky. Lamech and his generation brought forth the "natural" rain in the days of Noah to be destroyed. Could the current generation bring on the "spiritual" rain of the Holy Spirit and be saved? What do the Sons of Issachar discern?

"As it was in the days of Noah, so will it be at the coming of the Son of Man."

Matthew 24:37

Now we will examine more closely and break down the symbols and meanings of the year 5777, *"Hei, Zayin, Zayin, Zayin!"* Triple Zayin, first of all, is very unique and quite rare for there to be three sevens in the same year. These three sevens will not be repeated again for a thousand years. What will this year hold for America? What do the Sons of Issachar discern?

The letter _Hei-_ The fifth letter the Hebrew alphabet, pronounced, "Hay." "Hei" has a Gematria numerical value of five. The number five symbolizes God's grace, goodness, and favor toward humans. The pictograph of the letter "Hei" looks like a man with his arms raised speaking. Out of His mouth come divine breath, revelation, and light. "Hei" is a picture of the presence of God within the human heart. His spirit transforms, opens the heart of the broken, and is a picture of God indwelling in the believer. In the New Testament, the number five represents grace, and the five-fold ministry of the Church mentioned in Ephesians 4:11, namely those of apostles, prophets, evangelists, pastors, and teachers.

The letter _Zayin_ – The seventh letter of the Hebrew alphabet, pronounced "ZAH-een." The Gematria number of seven is linked to "completion or perfection" and is considered the highest sacred number in Bible Scriptures. There are seven days of creation, seven days a week, and seven feasts of Israel. Joshua marched seven times around Jericho, the Menorah has seven branches, and in Revelations 1:20, Jesus spoke of seven churches.

In the pictograph of the letter, "Zayin" is the picture of a "sword." The letter Zayin is one of the Hebrew letters that uses a decorative crown on top of the letter, forming a crown on the head. It looks like a sword or a scepter with a crown on its head. The rabbinical interpretation is that it can represent the "crowning of a leader." It can also represent war or a struggle.

Interesting to me, the word Zayin has the Gematria number of "67." This immediately makes me think of 1967. What happened in 1967? A Jubilee year, along with the Six-Day War in Israel and the Charismatic Movement in the United States started when "living water" was poured out by the Holy Spirit.

Zayin is also a paradoxical word since it can mean swift-weapon or sword, to clash or divide, battle or war raging, returning to the light, exposing what is concealed in the darkness. Zayin also comes from the root word that means "substance" or "nourishment" and can represent a weapon of the spirit like the

"Word of God." This could mean the battle of the clashing of heaven and hell, dividing the light from the darkness with the "clashing of swords." Fierce spiritual warfare can ensue. This collision has already started publicly in America's political arena with the conflict of ideologies.

Most definitely, the clashing of heaven and hell is showing up in the conflict of political ideologies on front lines of the political storm overtaking America. Spiritual warfare is erupting in our institutions. We as a country will not continue if Christians continue to be divided. There are demonic spirits being dispatched by the enemy to battle Christians in this election cycle. Many are so easily manipulated through media mind control. They use tactics such as sound bites, talking heads, and an onslaught of progressive liberal ideologies. It is baked every day into our entertainment by Hollywood elites.

However, we as Christians can easily win this warfare and nourish ourselves with the truth from the Word of God. Studying His Word will have an affect on us as we walk every day in faith.

"Depart from me, ye evildoers: for I will keep the commandments of my God."

Psalm 119:115

"Study to show thyself approved unto God, a workman that needeth not to be ashamed, rightly dividing the word of truth."

2 Timothy 2:15

As we consume or eat the bread of the Word of God, it will become a sword in your mouth as you speak authority and defeat the enemy. Like a soldier, boldness will overcome fear through the power of intimacy with Jesus Christ. I am reminded of a verse in scripture.

"For the Word of God is quick, and powerful, and sharper than any two-edged sword, piercing even to the dividing asunder of

soul and spirit, and of the joints and marrow, and is a discerner of the thoughts and intents of the heart."

Hebrews 4:12

In all history, there has been only one nation like America, founded by those seeking religious freedom and liberties to worship. It was established and dedicated to the proposition that we were all created equal and endowed by God with certain unalienable rights; we are One Nation under God.

I pray God can deliver and prosper us in peace and will raise up another generation in revival. The church must reestablish influence, especially in the minds of millennials. She must be the shining light to the world once again from our shores, transforming America from darkness, disobedience, and indifference. We must be brought back into the light from darkness and despair. The time is now to walk in the blessings of Jesus Christ, restore our access to the living water that does not run dry, but cleanses us and removes that which is not of God. Amen!

THE JUBILEE OF 1917-18

"And ye shall hallow the fiftieth year, and proclaim liberty throughout the land unto all the inhabitants thereof; it shall be a Jubilee unto you; and ye shall return every man unto his possession, and ye shall return every man unto his family."

Leviticus 25:10

The foundation of the *Sabbath Jubilee Cycle* of fifty years has been introduced in previous sections. Just as we surveyed the last Four Blood Moon Tetrads, we will look back at the last *three* Jubilee cycles as they relate to Israel and America. We will look at them as they continue to show an American spiritual connection with Israel. We will discover patterns within these cycles that may help to reveal future prophetic *set time* events. We'll first explore the 1917-18 and 1966-67 Jubilee cycles and reveal patterns and conclusions for the 2015-16 Jubilee.

Let's begin by examining America's *first* Jubilee cycle *after* support for a Jewish National Homeland at the end of World War I. The United States entry into World War I came in April 1917, after two and a half years of public protests; racial divide was expanding as the Ku Klux Klan (KKK) held rallies, parades, and marches around the country. Klan membership exceeded four million people nationwide.

Efforts made by President Woodrow Wilson to keep the United States neutral during the war ended in early 1917. Germany's decision on January 31, 1917, to target neutral shipping in a designated war-zone became the immediate cause of the entry of the United States into the war.

Five American merchant ships went down in March of 1915; the public was outraged. The terrorist attack and sinking of the passenger liner *RMS Lusitania* in May 1915 by Germany off the coast of England killed 1,198 people including 128 Americans. America paid much more attention to the war after the attack. The sinking of the Lusitania had a strong effect on public opinion because of the deaths of American civilians.

President Wilson asked Congress for *"a war to end all wars"* that would make the world safe for democracy. The first and most important decision was the size of the army. When the United States entered the war, the army stood at 200,000, hardly enough to have a decisive impact in Europe.

On May 18, 1917, a draft was imposed, and the numbers were increased rapidly. Initially, the expectation was that the United States would mobilize an army of one million. The number, however, would go much higher. Overall some 4,791,172 Americans would serve in World War I. Under the command of Major General *John J. Pershing*, some 2,084,000 would reach France, and 1,390,000 would see active combat.

When the war began, the American economy was in recession. But a 44-month economic boom ensued from 1914 to 1918, first as Europeans began purchasing United States goods for the war and later as the United States itself joined the battle. The long period of United States neutrality made the ultimate conversion of the economy to a wartime basis easier than it otherwise would have been. Real plant and equipment were added, and because they were added in response to demands from other countries already at war, they were added precisely in those sectors where they would be needed once America entered the war.

Although the United States was actively involved in World War I for only nineteen months, from April 1917 to November 1918, the mobilization of the economy was extraordinary. Over four million Americans served in the armed forces, and the economy turned out a vast supply of raw materials and munitions. Entry into the war in 1917 unleashed massive national production from civilian goods to war goods.

According to Hugh Rockoff of Rutgers University, between 1914 and 1918, some three million people were added to the military and half a million to the government. Government statistics show overall, unemployment declined from 7.9 percent to 1.4 percent in this period, in part because workers were drawn to new manufacturing jobs and because the military draft had removed many young men from the civilian labor force.

Companies were able to expand their reach around the world, and domestic consumption increased rapidly during the 1920's, hence the name "The Roaring 20s." With Britain weakened after the war, New York emerged as London's equal, if not her superior, in the contest to be the world's leading financial center.

The legacies after World War I were great for the American Economy. America had become a worldwide superpower both militarily and economically. Before the war began, the United States was a net debtor in international capital markets, but following the war, the United States began investing large amounts internationally, taking on the role traditionally played by Britain and other European countries.

America's post World War I economic boom was based on new industrial manufacturing technology. Returning soldiers naturally increased demand for goods and services. Additionally, wages increased causing the economy to grow. Prior to the war, much of the economy and labor force lived in rural areas. Rural agricultural economies collapsed and had to adjust as returning soldiers left the farm for higher wages in industrial factories.

America joined the war late; this meant that America was not crippled economically by massive debt, allowing her markets to expand into other countries, thus increasing economic growth. America lent large amounts of money to the Allies. This put America on a very strong economic footing by the end of the war in the form of lower taxes and tariffs on foreign imports.

New electrical goods such as washing machines came into demand. The chemical industry created new materials, which in turn created more jobs required to produce them. Ford and

General Motors grew in size as the automobile industry introduced new technologies and manufacturing techniques. Prices fell due to the assembly-line; this allowed the price of the *Ford Model T* fall in price from $850 to $260.

Total production of American industry increased by 50% in the 1920's, and while this was occurring, wages were steady or on the rise. People could afford to buy more goods, increasing the demand further and growing the economy. America was rich in fertile land, iron, and other such raw materials. This allowed primary business to easily and quickly add wealth into the American economy.

World War I, and particularly the War in the Middle-East, resulted in the beginning of the prophetic restoration of the land of Israel with America's help. The United States was indeed blessed economically after entry in the War.

The entry and participation by the United States in the war inevitably helped the Allies in Europe defeat the *German, Austro-Hungarian,* and *Ottoman Empires.* It allowed the British Empire's Egyptian Expeditionary Force under General *Edmund Allenby* to drive out the Turks from the Eastern Mediterranean. Four hundred years of Ottoman Empire Rule of the Middle-East was ended.

The *League of Nations* (Belgium, Britain, France, Greece, Italy, and Japan) divided the territory, formerly under Ottoman Empire, into new entities, called *mandates.* The mandates would be administered like "trusts" by the British and French, under supervision of the League, until such time as the inhabitants were believed by League members to be ready for independence and self-government. Soon after in November of 1917, the British Foreign Secretary Minister pledged support for establishment of a Jewish National Homeland in Palestine.

The *Balfour Declaration* was a letter by Foreign Secretary Arthur James Balfour, proclaiming a Jubilee for liberty throughout the land for the Jews. The Balfour Declaration set the forthcoming vision for the future nation of Israel and sparked waves of Jewish migration.

The mandate territories were Syria and Lebanon, awarded to France; Iraq and a new entity called Palestine was placed under British control. The British decided to carve out a new entity west of the Jordan River called the *British Mandate in Palestine*. In July 1922, the League of Nations ratified the mandate arrangement. This set the groundwork that would later lead to Israel's Independence; after the mandate expired on May 15, 1948.

THE JUBILEE OF 1966-67

Let's continue by surveying the Jubilee cycle of 1966-67. This was the *second* Jubilee cycle which occurred *after* support for a Jewish National Homeland. The Six-Day War was fought between June 5 -10, 1967. Once again, war in the Middle-East resulted in a major biblical prophetic restoration event during a Jubilee Sabbath Year for the State of Israel. Let's review, investigate, and find out how it happened. Furthermore, let's understand its importance.

Two future pivotal leaders were also elected in 1967; Ronald Reagan, a former movie actor, is inaugurated the new governor of California. Later elected as President of the United States, he would also serve as a close friend of Israel in the future. Moshe Dayan is elected Defense Minister of the Israel Defense Forces. He was commander of the Jerusalem front in the 1948 Arab–Israeli War and Chief of Staff of the Israel Defense Forces (1953–58) during the 1956 Suez Crisis.

Dayan did not take part in most of the planning before the Six-Day War of June 1967; however, he personally oversaw the capture of East Jerusalem during the June 5 -7 fighting. He wore an eye-patch and became to the world a fighting symbol of the new state of Israel.

The battle started when Israel responded to a build-up of Arab forces along its borders and launched preemptive simultaneous attacks against Egypt and Syria. Jordan subsequently entered the battle, but the Arab coalition was no match for Israel's proficient armed forces.

In six days of fighting, Israel occupied the Gaza Strip and the Sinai Peninsula of Egypt, the Golan Heights of Syria, and the West Bank an Arab sector of East Jerusalem. Both had previously been under Jordanian rule. By the time the United Nations cease-fire took effect on June 11, Israel had more than doubled its size. Israel had proved beyond question that it was the region's preeminent military power. The true fruits of victory came in claiming the Old City of Jerusalem from Jordan. Many wept while bent in prayer at the Western Wall of the *Second Temple*.

In the United States during most of the early 1960s, the American economy was passing through the phase of average prosperity. But starting in 1965, the industrial cycle entered the "boom" phase. In the mid-1960s, this transition was facilitated by government economic policies. One of the most effective was the Kennedy-Johnson "tax cut" of 1964.

The War in Vietnam did mean that a growing portion of the industrial capacity and labor power of the American economy had to be devoted to meet the needs of the war against Vietnam. This was on top of the already high level of "cold war" military expenditures.

When added to the effects of the Kennedy-Johnson "tax cut," the result was that United States industry had less excess capacity and unemployed labor power than at any time since the early 1950s. From 1965 onward, American industry could no longer increase production as fast as demand was growing at the existing price level, causing inflation to start to rise.

The immediate years after President Nixon's election, the unification of Jerusalem, and the Jubilee of 1966-67, according to the United States Bureau of Economic Analysis, saw that the GDP average growth rate for the United States from 1967-73 was 3.57%.

The end result with the Six-Day War victory marked the reunification and annexation of East Jerusalem as the Jewish capital of Israel for the first time since 70 AD. Jerusalem was reunited and restored on June 7, 1967. So why is this important? According to Biblegateway.com, the name Jerusalem is mentioned 810 times in the King James Version of the Bible: 661 times in the Old Testament and 149 times in the New Testament. God promised the restoration of Jerusalem in Zechariah 8:4-8. The Jews will once again re-occupy the city of Jerusalem and dwell in the streets. They shall be His people and He their God. Fulfilling Bible prophecy, the Jewish people miraculously retook the capital city in a stunning victory.

However, in the future, Jerusalem, the eternal capital of Israel will be the burden of the world, trembling unto all people around it. It will be the epicenter of world controversy. All the nations of the world will come together against Israel over the issue of the control of Jerusalem (Zechariah 12:1-3). Why is this so?

Jerusalem is significant to a number of religious traditions, including *Judaism, Christianity, and Islam*, which all consider it a holy city. Some of the most sacred places for each of these religions are found in Jerusalem, and the one shared between all three is the *Temple Mount*.

Jerusalem is one of the most ancient capitals of the world, continually populated by the Jewish people for more than 3,000 years. Jerusalem in Judaism is what Rome is to Roman Catholicism. For the Jews, Jerusalem is the place where Abram paid tithes to the *King-Priest Melchizedek*. It is the *City of David*, the capital of a glorious past where *Solomon's First Temple* stood as the great house built to honor the God of Abraham, Isaac, and Jacob. Jerusalem has been the holiest city in Judaism for praise and worship and is the ancestral and spiritual homeland of the Jewish people since 1,800 BC.

God said, *"But I have chosen Jerusalem, that my name might be there; and have chosen David to be over my people"* (2 Chronicles 6:6). King David made Jerusalem his capital as the First Kingdom of Israel over 3,000 years ago. He was succeeded by his son, King Solomon, who is known to have built the *First Temple* for the worship of God on Mount Moriah. In 1 Kings 5:5, King Solomon said that God promised his father David, *"Thy son, whom I will set upon thy throne in thy room, he shall build a house unto my name."*

God designated "Jerusalem" His Holy Capital City, the place where He chose to put His name (1 Kings 11:36). God chose Jerusalem as His own people from all the tribes (Judah the tribe of David) of Israel (1 Kings 11:32). All the nations will come against Jerusalem in a final cataclysmic showdown; God will save the tents of Judah first and glorify the House of David. The House of David shall be as God, as the angel of the LORD before them. God will seek to destroy all the nations that come against Jerusalem (Zechariah 12:7-9). God is a promise maker and a promise keeper, and His covenants are eternal. As long as there are a moon and stars in the heavens, He will always be with Israel.

"My covenant will I not break, nor alter the thing that is gone out of my lips. Once have I sworn by my holiness that I will not lie unto David. His seed shall endure for ever, and his throne as the sun before me. It shall be established for ever as the moon, and as a faithful witness in heaven."

Psalm 89:34-37

For Christians, it is the site of the death and resurrection of Jesus Christ. It was here that Jesus was crucified nearly 2,000 years ago and rose from the dead three days and three nights later just as He had foretold.

Jesus also told His disciples that He would visibly return to Jerusalem. In a message He gave while overlooking Jerusalem from the *Mount of Olives*, He explained that *"Immediately after the tribulation of those days the sun will be darkened, and the moon will not give its light; the stars will fall from heaven, and the powers of the heavens will be shaken. Then the sign of the Son of Man will appear in heaven, and then all the tribes of the earth will mourn, and they will see the Son of Man coming on the clouds of heaven with power and great glory."*

Matthew 24:29-30

Jerusalem is also considered sacred in Islamic tradition, along with the cities Mecca and Medina. Islamic tradition holds that the Islamic prophet Muhammad visited the city in a dream. The *Dome of the Rock* is an Islamic shrine in Jerusalem, built on the Temple Mount. This is where it is said to be where Muhammad ascended into heaven on his horse "Barrack" and was given the *second pillar of Islam*, to pray five times a day.

During its long history, Jerusalem has been attacked 52 times, captured and recaptured 44 times, besieged 23 times, and destroyed twice. The oldest part of the city was settled in the 4th millennium BC, making Jerusalem one of the oldest cities in the world. Jerusalem has accomplished a very important role in its bloody history and will again with the fulfillment of biblical prophecy with the return of Jesus Christ.

The Old Testament prophet Zechariah tells what will happen in the future in Zechariah 14:1-2, *"Behold, the day of the LORD is cometh, and thy spoil shall be divided in the midst of thee. For I will gather all nations against Jerusalem to battle; and the city shall be taken, and the houses rifled, and the women ravished, and half of the city shall go into captivity, and the residue of the people shall not be cut off from the city."*

The prophet further tells us in Zechariah 14:3-4 the vindication of the LORD for those who come against His people, *"Then the LORD will go forth, and fight against those nations, as when He fought in the day of battle. And His feet shall stand in that day upon the Mount of Olives, which is before Jerusalem on the east, and the Mount of Olives shall cleave in the midst thereof toward the east and the west, and there shall be a very great valley; and half of the mountain shall remove toward the north and half of it toward the south."* (See also Micah 1:3-4).

Also Zechariah 14:12 tells us the judgment of the nations for those that fight against his capital city, *"..the LORD will smite all that fought against Jerusalem; their flesh shall consume away while they stand upon their feet, and their eyes shall consume away in their holes, and their tongue shall consume away in their month."* (See also Joel 3:2).

It's one of the great paradoxes: for the "Prince of Peace" to bring an end to violence and strife; He has to fight a war. Mankind will initially see Jesus Christ not as the Savior, but as an invader. And it's in the area around Jerusalem that this catastrophic battle will take place. Jerusalem will then become the capital city of a one world government, not organized by the United Nations or similar organization, but established by Jesus Christ, the Son of God.

THE JUBILEE OF 2015-16

The foundation has now been positioned for the modern-day Sons of Issachar to understand Jubilee and what it may bring. We will review the last two Jubilee cycles as I have with the Four Blood Moon Tetrads and see if there is indeed an American and Israel spiritual connection. Let's start with a review of the commonalities with the 1917-18 and 1966-67 Jubilee cycles first before we discover what God may have in store for the world *after* the 2015-16 Jubilee cycle, *"a trump-blast of liberty."*

"And ye shall hallow the fiftieth year, and proclaim liberty throughout the land unto all the inhabitants thereof; it shall be a Jubilee unto you; and ye shall return every man unto his possession, and ye shall return every man unto his family."

Leviticus 25:10

In both instances, commonalities in both of the Jubilees of 1917-18 and 1966-67 coincided with war in the Middle-East. Both brought major biblical prophetic restoration events for Israel. America experienced war in both Jubilees that caused the United States to militarily enter foreign wars far from its shores (World War I and Vietnam). The economies were stagnant at the start of both Jubilees with much racial in the streets. Is there a pattern forming?

Like previously shown, God established patterns for times and seasons that are found throughout the Bible. The Jubilee cycle of 2015-16 was the *third* Jubilee cycle for America *after* support of the Balfour Declaration by Foreign Secretary Arthur James Balfour, *"proclaiming liberty throughout the land"* for a homeland for the Jewish people in 1917. Again, *three* represents perfection throughout the Bible also meaning completion and unity.

Can you see the pattern of the **"American's Jubilee Cycle?"** Did you see God's pattern with the *Tetrads*? Let's start with what is happening in America currently with the 2015-16 cycles and compare it to the 1917-18 and 1966-67 Jubilees and see if we are indeed repeating the pattern.

The first pattern we find with the Jubilees is the United States is at war, America's participation in both World War I in 1917, and the War in Vietnam in 1966. America in 2016 continues the Global War on Terror against Radical Islam. ISIS has expanded rapidly during this Jubilee with Israel and the United States as its main target of opposition, yet again this is another connection that we have with Israel.

An additional pattern found in the Jubilee cycle is racial divide. In 1917, the Ku Klux Klan divided American Politics much like the Black Panther Party did in 1966. America is currently more racially divided than ever in this current Jubilee. It has to stop; it is tearing our country's people apart, socially and economically! A few cases have been blown out of proportion for some evil political purpose.

In this Jubilee, Black Lives Matter (BLM) has originated within Black political left-leadership. It intensified in Ferguson, Missouri where Michael Brown, an African-American male, was shot to death after an encounter with a white-male police officer. Officer, Darren Wilson, was dispatched after a robbery and assault was reported in a nearby convenience store where Michael Brown was described.

Officer Wilson's account was that when he attempted to question Michael Brown, he was attacked. There was a struggle with Brown attempting and almost succeeding in gaining possession of Officer Wilson's weapon. Due to the struggle, the weapon discharged, slightly wounding Brown. Wilson, fearing for his life during the struggle, ultimately shot and killed Brown when Brown turned and charged at him.

The day after the fatal shooting of Michael Brown, protests and riots began. As the details of the original shooting event emerged, police established curfews and deployed riot squads to maintain order. Along with peaceful protests, rioters burned and looted businesses in the vicinity of the original shooting. According to media reports, there was police militarization when dealing with protests in Ferguson.

After several months of deliberation, a grand jury decided not to indict Officer Wilson for any criminal charges in relation to the incident. The Ferguson unrest sparked a vigorous debate in the United States about the relationship between law enforcement officers and African Americans, the militarization of the police, and the Use of Force.

Since Ferguson, participants in the movement have demonstrated for the removal of the Confederate Flag, and a number of memorials to the Confederate States of America were vandalized with graffiti. Expanding beyond street protests, BLM has expanded to activism on American college campuses, such as the 2015–16 University of Missouri protests.

In July 2016, a BLM protest was held in Dallas, Texas that was organized to protest the deaths of Alton Sterling and Philando Castile. At the end of the peaceful protest, Micah Xavier Johnson, an African-American male, opened fire in an ambush, killing five police officers and wounding seven others and two civilians. The gunman was then killed by a robot-delivered bomb. Before he died, according to police, Johnson said that "he was upset about Black Lives Matter," and that "he wanted to kill white people, especially white officers."

Beginning in August of 2016, several professional athletes have participated in National Anthem protests. The protests began in the National Football League (NFL) after Colin Kaepernick of the San Francisco 49ers sat during the anthem.

It saddens me as President Obama has helped fan the flames of the racial divide for political gain. I am not surprised by recent polls which show that Americans believe race relations are worsening even though the president of the United States is himself an

African-American male. He bends so far backward to avoid giving offense, even to those who richly deserve offending.

When the next president is sworn in, Obama will leave office without having healed the nation's festering racial or economic wounds. He will not have made them better; but rather worse. Obama's socialist policies, the *Affordable Care Act*, *anti-business regulation*, and *tax increases* over the last eight years, have lowered wages for all Americans and increased unemployment and poverty especially in the Black Community. Ninety-five million workers remain out of the workforce since he came into office. Home ownership is the lowest since 1949. According to the United States Bureau of Economic Analysis, the Real GDP Growth Rate under Obama from 2009-2016 has averaged 1.63%, the lowest since President Herbert Hoover.

President Obama will become the first president since Herbert Hoover not to serve during a year in which the growth in real GDP was at least 3%. The United States has gone a record ten straight years (2006-2016) without a year in which the growth in real GDP was at least 3%.

Other patterns I found within the Jubilee cycle were "tax cuts" and economic growth. I pray this happens with the next presidency! Halleluiah! Don't you? However, let me ask, what is missing in the pattern from the Jubilee cycles of 1917-18 and 1966-67 to complete the cycle of 2015-16? What can the Sons of Issachar discern?

The answer could be threefold: War in the Middle East, a major biblical prophetic restoration event in Israel, and God's anointed being placed in the White House to serve and protect the State of Israel. I'm not saying God told me there would be a War in the Middle East; I'm just showing you that it's in the pattern. What could the prophetic restoration event be in Israel?

Will America indeed have a "Jubilee" of restoration for leadership and management of our land with this presidential election? Is it America's *set time* in this Jubilee cycle for the United States to be led by Christian Leadership again? Can the campaign slogan, "Make America Great Again" be a reference to the Jubilee? Is it America's *set time* for a major move of the Holy Spirit? I'll explain more in the next section.

However, in the beginning of this text, I mentioned the "supernatural revelation" download God and placed in my spirit for America's future. He showed me America will indeed experience a Jubilee restoration like Israel. Israel's spiritual heritage is the land. Israel has restored what was theirs from the beginning (1917, 1948, and 1967). I have shown many examples how America, the Jewish people, and Israel have been spiritually connected and linked together since our discovery.

America's spiritual heritage has been, "One Nation under God." We have been the "Great Gentile Nation" that has spread the Gospel of Jesus Christ around the world and continues to do so. America has been the nation, "the light between the oceans" that spreads praise and worship which illuminates most of the Gospel of Jesus Christ to the world. We have been the nation that has supported the Jewish people and the State of Israel more than any other. God has blessed us more than any nation because of this.

I believe God will give America one more chance with the body of Christ in a narrow window to preach the true Gospel of Jesus Christ. Here is what I felt in my spirit when asked about the presidential election; I sensed it while driving, ***"He turned it."*** Restoration of our land will indeed return as a Christian Nation under the next president and "Make America Great Again!"

THE PRESIDENTIAL ELECTION OF 2016

Let's review the summary of the Jubilee Sabbath Year as God intended and get a clue to what God is unveiling. The Jubilee is set for the future coming of Yeshua, as His reign will be one continual Jubilee. Justice and truth will reign with *"a trump-blast of liberty."* It will obtain liberty and break all oppression.

God has placed in motion the Jubilee and America's *set time.* The 45th President of the United States, with *"a trump-blast of liberty"* will be Donald Trump. In 1948 and 1968, God put in the White House men with a heart for Israel and helped them in their time of need. God will do it again with Donald Trump.

In ancient Israel, the Jubilee had a special impact on the ownership and management of land. According to the Book of Leviticus, slaves and prisoners would be freed, debts would be forgiven, and the mercies of God would be particularly manifested. *"That fiftieth year shall be a Jubilee to you. you shall not sow, neither reap that which grows of itself, nor gather from the undressed vines. For it is a Jubilee; it shall be holy to you. You shall eat of its increase out of the field. In this Year of Jubilee each of you shall return to his property."*

Leviticus 25:11-13

Would you not say that America's original rightful owners and managers were Christians? How about today's leadership in America? Have Christians lost their influence within the United States? Many of our *Founding Fathers* spread the Word of Jesus and enjoyed religious freedom and liberty. Recall our nation's dedication to God by George Washington? How about the Liberty Bell? This further shows how we connect to both the God of Israel and the Jubilee.

Since the passing of the Johnson Amendment in 1954, ministers and pastors have been quiet, politically speaking. Fearful of losing tax-exempt status and bringing attention to themselves, they have watered down their messages to *"itching ears"* (2 Timothy 4:1-5).

146

In the decades following, believers have become passive and accommodating. As a result, prayer was removed from school, and the legalized abominations of abortion and gay marriage were upheld by the United States Supreme Court.

This has further encouraged many on the political left to attack religious freedoms even more, as they are ferocious to limit the voice of Christians in the public political arena. Jesus tells us what power and authority we have in Luke 10:19, *"I give unto you power to tread on serpents and scorpions, and over all the power of the enemy; and nothing shall by any means hurt you."*

Christians in America have seceded enough to the liberal left which has divided our country. Mark 3:25 tells us, *"A house divided against itself cannot stand."* The proof is in scripture that we have the power to defeat the enemy. It is time for all believers to stand together and be one voice. America will be either ruled by the Bible or by the bayonet! We are the generation that can break the chains of America's despair. It is up to us, *"the remnant,"* to stand and reclaim our spiritual heritage for revival, humble ourselves, and we must ask God in prayer to heal and restore our land. It's the only way to push back the enemy.

"If my people, which are called by my name, shall humble themselves, and pray, and seek my face, and turn from their wicked ways; then will I hear from heaven, and will forgive their sin, and will heal their land."

2 Chronicles 7:14

How will God restore our land and leadership? Jubilee! I believe God placed in my spirit that Republican Presidential Nominee, Donald Trump is anointed for this *"set time."* Many still can't believe this man ever won the nomination. God's Hand is certainly on this man. The most astonishing aspect of all is the fact that God's plan isn't always what God's people choose. I'm a believer that God directs our steps, *"...he orders the steps of a good man."* Trump was raised up by God to serve His purpose.

147

God is indeed making statements by what He is doing. It's the only thing that makes sense! A record number of Christians and Evangelicals will turn out for Trump on Election Day and turn the tide. He will usher in God's Jubilee for America and restoration with a *"trump-blast of liberty."*

God placed in my spirit the 2016 presidential election will be a lot like the 1948 presidential election. I kept feeling in my spirit when asked about the election, ***"1948! 1948! 1948!"*** The 2016 presidential election will be very similar and parallel to the election of 1948. Remember the earlier section about Harry S. Truman? The media said he couldn't win either! Trump's win will mirror Truman's victory in 1948. America will be stunned once again when they wake up the day after the election. What? Trump won?

The pattern revealed within the Tetrads of 1949-50 and 1967-68 showed that God affected presidential elections to help Israel. I believe God blessed His servant Harry S. Truman with the biggest upset win in American Presidential History in the election of 1948. God helped to elevate, the Quaker, Richard M. Nixon to the White House in 1968 for the future benefit of Israel. In both elections, God placed into the White House, men with a heart for God's chosen people.

However, America as a whole has forgotten our spiritual heritage and blessing. We have forgotten our connection to the Jewish people as the world continues to isolate Israel and wants to divide her land. The assault on Israel will become a climax among the nations during the next presidency for sure. America must come to her aid and support for our very own survival as well. In 2016, God will place in the White House again a man with a heart for Israel.

Donald Trump, "God's Trumpet" will sound off and champion Israel like no other since Harry S. Truman. He will reaffirm the unbreakable bond between the United States and the Jewish State.

Israel Prime Minister Benjamin Netanyahu said, "His leadership will make the Israel-America alliance ever greater."

However, the battle isn't going to stop after the election. I speculate after the election there will be further chaos accelerating the division of light and darkness with "fierce spiritual warfare" across the nation. Opposition will battle God's people and His anointed with the "clashing of swords" in 5777.

Like Jubilee, restoration will return to religious institutions and churches when Donald Trump keeps his promise to repeal the Johnson Amendment as president. At that point, all the evil demonic spirits from the pits of the media and the liberal elite-left will become "disjointed" upon his election and attack him and his supporters. Watching the legacy media will be like watching *Linda Blair* and *Max von Sydow* of the movie *Exorcist* every night on cable. Satan knows that he has but a short time. However, all the forces of darkness cannot stop what God has ordained (Isaiah 14:27).

It will be God's divine decree that His appointed season for blessing the church has arrived. Churches in America will for a brief time have a "window of grace" and will be allowed to preach the true gospel of Jesus Christ freely across the nation in revival with the help of a Holy Spirit. Many souls will be saved for the Kingdom of Jesus Christ while the window of grace is open. Let's get to work!

OUTPOURING: THE JUBILEE REVIVAL

"And ye shall know that I am in the midst of Israel and that I am the LORD your God, and none else: and my people shall never be ashamed. And it shall come to pass afterward, that I will pour out my spirit upon all flesh; and your sons and your daughters shall prophecy, your old men shall dream dreams, your young men shall see visions."

Joel 2:27-28

God promised there is coming a praise and worship generation that will lead the way (Judah), shoulder great pressures, do miracles and rebuild what was torn down or broken. They will not be afraid and will instead be courageous; they will win souls for Jesus Christ and help break the chains that will finally set all free.

In the Tetrads, I showed the pattern for spiritual outpourings, tax cuts, economic expansion and presidential elections cycles. In the Jubilee cycles, patterns revealed violence and racial divide, war and prophetic restoration for Israel. The Tetrads and the Jubilee patterns converge together to form unique patterns.

One of them is spiritual outpouring; the ***"Third Major Wave of Rain"*** is upon us. We will celebrate the outpouring of the Holy Spirit as a life-transforming experience, similar to the love of God that is poured into one's heart and is received through surrender to the Lordship of Jesus Christ.

The Holy Spirit, with a fresh wind, will reignite revival. This recovery of *Pentecost* will be an experience of Jubilee, raising the remnant out of the darkness, and experience freedom from the bondage of sins into the marvelous light of being sons and daughters of a loving Father.

Isaiah 35 tells us water will gush in the wilderness and the parched land will rejoice, then will the eyes of the blind be opened and the ears of the deaf unstopped. The lame will leap like a deer, and the mute will shout for joy! The ransomed of the LORD (those who are delivered from the guilt and power of sin, and from every kind of spiritual bondage, whether it is to the devil, the world, or the flesh) shall return to Zion with songs and everlasting joy and be restored to their own land (Jubilee).

Do the Sons of Issachar hear the sound of abundance of rain (I Kings 8:41)? The infrastructure of revival is being laid under the surface and is starting to break out. When God snaps his fingers and pours out His Spirit, what a marvel it will be when the spiritual drought is washed away by His rain.

God placed in my spirit that America will indeed have a "Jubilee Revival" and restoration will return to our land. God further placed in my spirit that, *"The elect (the remnant) are going to see great provision for seven years to fulfill my harvest and Proclaim liberty throughout the land unto all the inhabitants thereof."*

"And shall not God avenge his own elect, which cry day and night unto him, though he bears long with them?"

Luke 18:7

We always see ourselves from the perspective of generational curses; however, we are now going to see the benefits of our family blood-lines. There's still a remnant of saints who believe in the "Power of the Blood." With the Blood of Jesus Christ, generational blessings are coming in the Jubilee! Think big!

God has chosen a remnant for this *"set time"* in America. Just as in Elijah's day, there is still today a remnant of believers who hold true to the teachings of Jesus. He is rising up His anointed remnant with a "Jubilee Revival." It will be the "Greatest Outpouring the World Has Ever Seen!" The Holy Spirit will pour into the sons and daughters like the Spirit of Elijah. *"There's fire on the mountain! It's raining in the high places!"*

"The elect are going to see great provision for seven years to fulfill my harvest." Some will see a double portion of prosperity

151

and blessings. A *Zebulun* type anointing will be placed upon those whom God has designated to be carriers of wealth, favor and financial support. They will see financial releases as God freely disperses "Supernatural Provision" to open doors to serve others. He can bring us into abundance. The newly ordained Sons of Issachar need to think big!

Others will have a *Judah* type anointing like a prevailing spirit of a young lion. Lions have no fear. They are the king of the beasts and have a "ruling anointing" that operates fearlessly, victoriously and in great authority. They will take the high ground and occupy it. God will send the Holy Spirit to anoint His people to raise them up in boldness and will be praised. Signs will follow them as they cast out devils, speak with new tongues, lay hands on the sick and heal them (see Mark 16:17-18).

Those who walk in the *Issachar* anointing will have close personal wisdom of the Word of God. With this anointing, those who are hungry for more of God's Word will be enabled to draw out hidden treasures. They will be leaders who have understanding of times and seasons, anointed with eyes to see, ears to hear, and a heart for compassion. They will be illuminated with understanding. The Sons of Issachar will know the timing of the Lord. God is going to impart revelation to them that was hidden from previous generations. The Sons of Issachar, knowing the timing of God and interpreting the times and seasons!

Just as the tribes of Israel worked together to do the will of God, so will they work together to enable the remnant of saints to do the same today. In Deuteronomy 33:18-19, we see the prophetic decree that both Zebulun and Issachar will call peoples to come up to the mountain of the LORD. There they will offer righteous sacrifices. They will draw out the abundance of the seas and the hidden treasures of the sand. The abundance of the seas and the hidden treasures are both spiritual and literal treasures of prosperity.

All *three* will need collaboration in order to work as "one." The wisdom of Issachar, the resources of Zebulun, and the fearlessness of Judah will together be well equipped to fulfill God's purpose. America has an unfinished assignment in the world. The time has come to harvest the nations, both Jew and Gentile!

This is God's response to prayer that will be used to set up and help many who will be in despair like in the time of Lamech and his generation. Churches will rise up to work to eliminate poverty in the inner cities. Help and refuge will come as the plans of previous blueprints that God gave many in the past to be implemented. Hundreds of thousands will be saved in America and the Middle East will experience revival too.

"And we know that all things work together for good to them that love God, to them who are the called according to His purpose."
Romans 8:28

The fires of salvation will sweep through Israel. God's Spirit will be poured out like never before in the Middle East, bringing in a harvest of new believers of Jesus Christ from among the Jewish people and the Muslim world. This will result in a great revival within Israel, especially among the youth.

"And I will pour upon the house of David, and upon the inhabitants of Jerusalem, the spirit of grace and of supplications: and they shall look upon me whom they have pierced, and they shall mourn for him, as one mourneth for his only son, and shall be in bitterness for him, as one that is in bitterness for his first-born."
Zechariah 12:10

People will rise up to carry out projects that will prepare for trouble ahead. The LORD is saying to His people to *"proclaim liberty throughout the land unto all the inhabitants thereof,"* so that they can help others to find their way. A great multitude of people will come out of the narrow place. God will prepare His people to maneuver through great financial hardships and provide necessary resources from the enemy. He will punish the enemies and prosper the remnant.

"...the wealth of the sinner is laid up for the just."
Proverbs 13:22

The wealth of the sinner will find its way into the hands of the righteous as God is in charge of wealth transfer. The reservoirs of the wicked will be drained into the hands of God's people to do His work (see Job 27:16-19).

Where the enemy has resisted our harvest in years past, we will see a multiplication of blessings. Doors will open supernaturally to the elect that no man can open. Opportunities will come our way that we never dreamed, imagined, or even thought to ask for. Provisions will enter from unexpected places.

Jubilee will uncover a "Great Wickedness in the Land," releasing the whistle blowers as corruption in our nation will be exposed. There will be a greater separation of light and darkness. That which is light is growing brighter, and that which is darker is being uncovered-it has no place to hide.

"He revealeth the deep and secret things: he knoweth what is in the darkness, and the light dwelleth with him."
Daniel 2:22

"For there is nothing covered, that shall not be revealed; neither hid, that shall not be known. Therefore, whatsoever ye have spoken in darkness shall be heard in the light; and that which ye have spoken in the ear in closets shall be proclaimed upon the housetops."
Luke 12:2-3

People will profess their confession of faith that has never been spoken out. Evil is about to be uncovered before all to see. We will know the difference between those who are in darkness and those who practice darkness. But know also that God is rising up an army of believers who will not be afraid to disarm, tear down, uproot and destroy those evil works.

The Lord has given us eyes to see and ears to hear what the Holy Spirit is saying to us. There will be much unveiled and many will come to a realization of the lies and deceit that have been told to us by the media and the political elite. There will an unveiling of secret agreements, things within the political arena and world terrorism. Much will be uncovered in the coming months. Some of it will shock many and confirm to others what has been at work under the surface.

God will also uncover within the church these things as a sign of the times where He himself will be dealing with whom He has previously warned. The churches whose foundations are not established firmly on the "Rock" will fall. Many will be stunned at the churches that fail because of the good front they have, but have refused to live in righteousness. The Holy Spirit will reveal their greed and idolatry to expose their sin. We will see many things during the course of Jubilee. We must pray for our nation, our leadership, and our divine protection under the sovereign Hand of God as we continue to become all that He is preparing in us.

CYRUS THE 45th PRESIDENT

The 45th President of the United States, with *"a trump-blast of liberty"* will be Donald Trump. Could there be a sign from God to proclaim America's Jubilee? Donald John Trump was born in Queens, New York on June 14th, 1946. If you move ahead 70 years from the date of his birth, it brings you to June 14, 2016. Moving forward another 7 months brings you to January 14, 2017, and moving forward another 7 days brings you to January 21, 2017. What does this mean? It means Donald Trump will be, 70 years, 7 months, and 7 days old (777) on his first full day in office. Trump will be inaugurated on January 20th, but his administration officially starts at midnight. How incredible is that? Is this a sign for America's set time?

These three sevens - 70 years, plus 7 months, plus 7 days are three sevens. This would happen during year 5777 on the Hebrew calendar. When Donald Trump wins the election, what about a sign for Israel? Donald Trump was 700 days old when Israel was born in a day on May 14th, 1948. When Israel was 77 days old, Donald Trump was 777 days old! Donald Trump will be elected on Israeli Prime Minister Benjamin Netanyahu's seventh year, seventh month, and seventh day in office. Very incredible indeed!

How about the Temple Mount area in Jerusalem covering 45 acres? Why only 45 acres? Could this be a reference to Cyrus as written in Isaiah 45? Will the 45th President of the United States be God's proponent for Israel and the *Third Temple*? Discern about that a little bit.

Time will tell but think about this awhile. Israel was born on May 14, 1948. When we add 70 years, plus 7 months, plus 7 days, this brings us to Friday, December 21, 2018. This is a Sabbath Day in Israel. It is the Winter Solstice, an astronomical phenomenon that marks the first day of winter. It is the shortest day with the least

156

amount of daylight and the longest in darkness of the year. What does the future hold? Discern the times Sons of Issachar.

Will a pattern arise with Donald Trump, the 45th President of the United States, in the Hebrew year 5777? Does his rise point prophetically to Isaiah 45:1-3? Will a prophetic pattern reveal that there is a strange destiny behind the rise of Donald Trump? Will he perform, in the same manner like Cyrus the King of Persia, be the leader who will deal positively with Israel; will he fulfill specific prophecies that are linked with Israel and the Jewish People?

"Thus saith the LORD, thy redeemer, and he that formed thee from the womb, I am the LORD that maketh all things; that stretcheth forth the heavens alone; that spreadeth abroad the earth by myself; That frustrateth the tokens of the liars, and maketh diviners mad; that turneth wise men backward, and maketh their knowledge foolish; That confirmeth the word of his servant, and performeth the counsel of his messengers; that saith to Jerusalem, Thou shalt be inhabited; and to the cities of Judah, Ye shall be built, and I will raise up the decayed places thereof: That saith to the deep, Be dry, and I will dry up thy rivers: That saith of Cyrus, He is my shepherd, and shall perform all my pleasure: even saying to Jerusalem, Thou shalt be built; and to the temple, Thy foundation shall be laid."

Isaiah 44:24-28

"Thus saith the LORD to his anointed, to Cyrus, whose right hand I have holden, to subdue nations before him; and I will loose the loins of kings, to open before him the two leaved gates; and the gates shall not be shut; I will go before thee, and make the crooked places straight: I will break in pieces the gates of brass, and cut in sunder the bars of iron: And I will give thee the treasures of darkness, and hidden riches of secret places, that thou mayest know that I, the LORD, which call thee by thy name, am the God of Israel."

Isaiah 45:1-3

I feel we are about to see long awaited prophetic events fulfilled in ways we can barely imagine. God has ordained Donald Trump for the times and seasons with a divine mission. Donald Trump has said, "I have felt that God has called me to be President." God called him; man did not. God personally is going to direct the actions of Donald Trump.

Like Cyrus, Trump loves Israel and the Jewish people. Israel is currently isolated and in danger of worldly events; the Iran Nuclear Deal, Hamas, Palestinians, ISIS, Turkey, Russia, Syria, and the United Nations all seem to be against the Jews. He will stand for peace in the Middle East and Israel.

Trump's victory will be due in part to his support of Israel. His campaign promise to move the United States Embassy from Tel Aviv to Jerusalem will result in officially recognizing the city as the eternal capital of Israel. The Jerusalem Embassy Act of 1995, passed congress but has been vetoed by every American President.

The pendulum will swing. The balance of the scales of Lady Justice will finally tilt equally for liberty and justice for all Americans. Trump will change the landscape in Washington DC for self-governance by the people. He will expose the darkest perversion of *pedophiles* in America like never before within the political-elite and the demon-possessed media. He will "drain the swamp" and expose the *deep state* and *shadow government*. He will build a protective wall on our southern border for homeland security. He will help to regain American economic prosperity. Trump's economic plan to rebuild America will start with "tax cuts" and rolling back the restrictive controlling regulations of the government for families and business.

He will begin to restore our military to a world superpower, seek energy independence, and repatriate corporate profits. All of this could see our GDP Growth Rate once again reach 4% and send the stock market to higher prosperity. The economy in the United States will be again the safe refuge for investments around the world. The result will create millions of new jobs for *"the people had a mind to work."*

He will appoint conservative judges to the Unites States Supreme Court. He will stand for the forgotten working man and will also stand for nationalism and independent thinking. Trump will be a threat to the elite ruling class - chosen and appointed by God for the containment of evil. He will hold back the tide and send the *"globalist and luciferians"* back on their heels.

Think about God's power shift with Trump. When the appointed are placed in leadership, their first line of business is to make sure the glory of the Lord is restored. Trump will stand for religious freedom and human rights, stemming the tide of persecuted Christians and Jews around the world. The Trump era will open up the door to the people of God globally to further advance the Kingdom. Christians must seize this window of grace while it is open.

Bondage will be broken as Trump suspends the Johnson Amendment and restores free speech with Jubilee, *"religious liberty"* for pastors and ministers. Trump will seek Godly council as he has already in place a Christian Leadership Council of 1,000 pastors and ministers. *"The ear that heareth the reproof of life abideth among the wise. He that refuseth instruction despiseth his own soul: but he that heareth reproof getteth understanding."*

Proverbs 15:31-32

"Blessed is the man that walketh not in the counsel of the ungodly, nor standeth in the way of sinners, nor sitteth in the seat of the scornful. But his delight is in the law of the Lord; and in his law doth he meditate day and night. And he shall be like a tree planted by the river of water, that bringeth forth his fruit in his season; his leaf also shall not wither; and whatsoever he doeth shall prosper."

Psalm 1:1-3

Donald Trump is open to the prophets and the prophetic word. There are good prophets of God surrounding him and speaking into his life. 2 Chronicles 36:22 says, *"Now in the first year of Cyrus king of Persia, that the Word of the Lord by the mouth of Jeremiah might be fulfilled, the Lord stirred up the spirit of Cyrus king of Persia, so that he made a proclamation throughout his entire kingdom, and also put it in writing, saying..."*

In the days lying ahead, what will Trump do? Will he restore (Jubilee) and rebuild America from decay? Can Donald Trump broker the Israeli-Palestinian deal of a lifetime? Will he decree building of the *Third Temple*? Could this be the cornerstone Trump-ism phrase, "the Art of the Deal" after his bestselling book of the same title?

If Trump really has a similar calling to Cyrus, could it be that God would use this real estate developer turned President to facilitate the greatest property development of modern time to rebuilding of the *Third Temple*? Could President Trump's strong pro-Israel stand be the game changer? What role would Russian President Vladimir Putin play in the mix? Could this be the major biblical restoration event for Israel that signals the *End of Days*? What do the Sons of Issachar discern?

Vladimir Putin's mother, *Maria Shelomova*, was a very kind, benevolent person and very dear to her son. On her death bed in 1998, it has been said Putin accepted Jesus Christ. On an official trip to Jerusalem in 2012, Putin paid a late-night visit to the Western Wall. When he arrived at the holy site, the Russian leader stood in silence for several minutes, offering up a personal prayer, after which he read Psalm from a Russian-Hebrew prayer book.

An Israeli bystander called out in Russian, "Welcome President Putin." Putin approached the man, who explained the importance of the Temple Mount and the Jewish Temple. Chadrei Chardim, an Orthodox Hebrew news site, reported that Putin responded,

"That's exactly the reason I came here, to pray for the Temple to be built again."

Putin also was honored in Bethlehem, and a street was named after him in 2012. According to the Jewish Telegraphic Agency, Putin is popular amongst the Russian Jewish community, who see him as a force for stability. His approach to religious policy has been characterized as one who supports religious freedoms. Putin regularly attends the most important services of the Russian Orthodox Church.

President Trump will visit Israel early in his presidency near the 50th Jubilee anniversary of the unification of Jerusalem. I hope he will pray for the peace and resolve of Israel at the Western Wall and then ascend to the Temple Mount and make the decree to build the *Third Temple*. At that point we will know it he is in the pattern of Cyrus.

If we fully want to understand the pattern of Cyrus and discern the order of future events, we must first ask. Who was Cyrus? What did he do to help "Make Israel Great Again?" What influence did he inspire?

Cyrus was one of the most important monarchs in the ancient world. Cyrus was a wise and remarkable ruler mentioned more than 30 times in the Bible as is identified as *Cyrus the Great, King of Persia* who reigned over Persia between 539 - 530 BC. He is important in Jewish history because it was under his rule that the Jews were first allowed to return to Israel after years of captivity with the conquering of Babylon in 539 BC.

Cyrus declared all the Jews held captive in Babylon were to be set free and allowed to return home to Jerusalem, as described in Ezra 1. Cyrus set in motion 50 years (a Jubilee) of national recovery for Israel. The *Cyrus Decree,* (Ezra 1:1-4) is the moment that heaven authorized for the return and restoration of God's people.

Revealing His sovereignty over all nations, God says of Cyrus in Isaiah 44:28, *"He is my shepherd and shall perform all my pleasure."* God's use as a *"shepherd"* for His people illustrates the truth of Proverbs 21:1, *"The king's heart is in the hand of the LORD, as the rivers of water: He turneth it whithersoever He will."*

Despite the fact the Persian King did not know the God of Israel, God appointed him by name with the mandate to fulfill God's divine purposes concerning the nation of Israel. Cyrus actively assisted the Jews in rebuilding the *Second Temple* in Jerusalem under *Ezra and Zerubbabel.* Cyrus restored the temple treasures that were taken by *Nebuchadnezzar* to Jerusalem and allowed building expenses to be paid from the royal treasury (Ezra 1:4-11, 6:4-5). Cyrus's generosity helped to restart temple worship practices that had languished during the years of the Babylonian Captivity.

Among the Jews exiled from Judah and later placed under the rule of Cyrus includes the prophet Daniel. We are told Daniel served until at least the third year of King Cyrus, approximately 536 BC (Daniel 10:1). Daniel likely had some personal involvement in the decree that was made in support of the Jews.

The *Jewish Historian Josephus* says that Cyrus was informed of the biblical prophecies written about him (Antiquities of the Jews, XI.1.2). The natural person to have shown Cyrus the scrolls was Daniel, a high-ranking official in Persia (see Daniel 6:28).

Besides his dealings with the Jews, Cyrus was perhaps the most influential figure in establishing human and civil rights, pioneering the religiously and ethically tolerance of ruling. He emphasized his own humanitarian nature with the freedom to choose religion.

Cyrus employed superb military generals and was himself a brilliant military strategist who viewed himself not as a conqueror, but more of a liberator of tyranny. He shied away from his ability to do harm to his enemies. He did not kill innocent people or enslave them. Cyrus perpetrated himself as a merciful and temperate conqueror and is remembered for his masterful art of diplomacy. His kingdom enjoyed economic growth unparalleled in Persian history. Cyrus was also an innovative builder with high standards. He built cities and rose up the decayed places. God used him to rebuild Jerusalem, and through him, the foundation would be laid to "Make Israel Great Again."

Unprecedented at that time, he allowed individual providences to govern themselves. He practiced religious tolerance and respect; native traditions and cultures stayed intact with the bridging of both Eastern and Western cultures. This made ruling efficient and inspired the populist years after his death.

Evidence from Babylon provides that Cyrus died around 530 BC in battle and that his son *Cambyses II* became king. Cambyses continued his father's policies and captured Egypt for the Empire, but he soon died after only seven years of rule. He was succeeded by an imposter posing as the son of Cyrus, *Bardiva*, who became the sole ruler of Persia for seven months until he was killed by *Darius the Great.*

Darius organized a new uniform monetary system, along with making *Aramaic* the official language of the empire. Darius' rule was marked by vast military expeditions. After consolidating his power at home, the Persian Empire reached its peak. Darius led military campaigns in Europe and Greece, conquering lands and expanding his empire. He also improved the legal and economic system and conducted impressive construction projects across the empire. Through these changes, the empire was centralized and unified. Darius is also mentioned in the Biblical books of Haggai, Zechariah, Ezra, and Nehemiah.

Nonetheless, in Jerusalem during the years following the Cyrus Decree, the exiles had much opposition. They were hindered from rebuilding the *Second Temple*, after having started the work, for a period of fifteen years quit (Ezra 4:24). In the second year of the reign of Darius, the prophet Haggai with a passionate and simple message from the Lord, called on the discouraged Jews to complete the temple (Haggai 1:8.) With all the remnant of the people, they obeyed the words of the Lord from prophet and resumed their task.

The Book of Ezra 6:1-11 describes the "second decree" which was to continue reconstruction of the Temple in Jerusalem, specifying financial support and supplies for the temple services. After a period of friction, the temple was finally completed in 516 BC, the sixth year of the reign of Darius and 70 years after the destruction of the *First Temple*. The *First Temple* was destroyed in 586 BC by Nebuchadnezzar; and until the completion of the *Second Temple* by Darius, the Jews were without a temple. Pay attention Sons of Issachar. Here is the clue.

It took TWO rulers to decree the building and completion of the *Second Temple* between Cyrus and Darius. Generous funding of the temple, by Darius, later gave him and his successors the support of the Jewish priesthood.

Years after the Cyrus Degree, enthusiasm of the people had dampened and many evil practices had crept into Jerusalem. King *Artaxerxes* was the grandson of Darius. He commissioned *Ezra*, a Jewish priest and scribe, by means of a letter of decree to take charge of the religious and civil affairs of the Jewish nation. According to the Bible, Ezra was a descendant of *Seraiah* (Ezra 7:1), the last High Priest to serve in the *First Temple* (2 Kings 25:18).

Nehemiah, the *cup-bearer* of the king (high ranking officer in the royal court) learning that the remnant in the province was in distress, returned to Jerusalem and found appalling conditions among the people. Artaxerxes made him the governor of Judah with a commission to rebuild Jerusalem and the walls. Once there, Nehemiah defied the opposition of Judah's enemies on all sides and rebuilt the walls within 52 days. This event is described in the Book of Nehemiah 4:6; he instituted the rebuilding of the walls of Jerusalem for *"the people had a mind to work."* He served twelve years as governor, during which he ruled with justice and righteousness.

He and Ezra were further used by God to bring about a "mighty revival" that turned the whole nation back to God. Great indeed was this revival that moved Israel back to God with the Feast of Tabernacles being restored. The account of this "great awakening" is found in the Book of Nehemiah, chapters 8 and 9. It was brought about by the reading of the Word of God (Torah) by Ezra to the people. In Nehemiah 8:8, *"So they read in the book, in the law of God distinctly, and gave them sense, and caused them to understand the reading."*

Does the biblical history of Cyrus and Darius foretell the future prophetic patterns of Trump and possibly Putin when it relates to the *Third Temple*? What do the Sons of Issachar discern? Will religious freedom on the Temple Mount for the Jews be enough of a human and civil rights issue for Trump to decree the Temple? Through him, will the foundation of the *Third Temple* be laid? We will all know in the realm of God's *set time*; in the meanwhile, pray for the peace Jerusalem.

THE THIRD TEMPLE

"Pray for the peace of Jerusalem, they shall prosper who love thee."

Psalm 122:6

"But you shall seek the LORD at the place which the LORD your God will choose from all your tribes, to establish His name there for His dwelling, and there you shall come."

Deuteronomy 12:5

The Temple Mount today covers about 45 acres with an elevation of 740 meters above sea level or about 2,430 feet. Why did God select this specific elevation? Is there a mystery to be revealed? Let's play with the numbers a little and see if we can find clues to God's divine meaning in His Word.

Using Strong's Hebrew Concordance, the 740th word listed is *Ariel*. It occurrences six times in the Bible in Isaiah 29 and is the symbolical name for Jerusalem as the city where David dwelt. It means "altar-hearth" or a place for burnt offerings. It can also mean "Lion of God." Wow! What a surprise that the 740th word in the concordance lexicon is about Jerusalem! What does the prophet Isaiah say about Ariel?

The prophet describes both the cause and cure of the spiritual blindness of Israel. In Isaiah 29:1-2, *"Woe to Ariel, to Ariel, the city where David dwelt! Add ye year to year; let them kill sacrifices. Yet I will distress Ariel, and there shall be heaviness and sorrow: and it shall be unto me as Ariel."*

Jerusalem had a high opinion of itself, was proud and prideful, resting on its spiritual heritage instead of its present reality. It lived for pleasures without a concern for God. The prophet Isaiah condemned religious formality, pointing out that their empty religion of routine to comply with custom and serving their own interest was not out of the reach of God's hand of judgement.

166

"Pride goes before the fall" (see Proverbs 16:18). Can the Sons of Issachar discern a message for America?

The prophet says in Isaiah 29:13, *"Wherefore the Lord said, Forasmuch as the people draw near me with their mouth, and with their lips do honor me but have removed their heart far from me, and their fear toward me is taught by the precept of men."* Jesus repeats the prophet Isaiah in Mark 7:6-8 as He called out hypocrites to the embodiment of the Pharisees and scribes.

Using <u>Strong's Hebrew Concordance,</u> now let's look up the 2,430th word. Could this be another reference to Jerusalem and the Temple Mount? The 2,430th word is *Cheylah* (khay-law). Used only once in the Bible meaning; bulwark, entrenchment, rampart, and fortress. Used in Psalm 48:13, *"Mark ye well her bulwarks, consider her palaces, that ye may tell it to the generation following."* This is a future messianic reference!

Psalm 48 is about the Songs of Zion for the Sons of Korah, who sang about the glory of the city of Jerusalem and the temple which has been delivered by God from her enemies. The city of God is praised and her attackers are defeated. Her people praise the LORD for His loving kindness!

Who were the Sons of Korah? The story of "Korah's Rebellion" is told in The Book of Numbers Chapter 16. Korah was from the tribe of Levi and rose up against Moses in the wildness. The leaders of the rebellion included a group headed by Korah and composed principally of Levites who were offended by the setting a part of the family of Aaron for the duties and privileges of the priesthood. Another group, headed by Abiram and Dathan, felt that they, rather than Moses, should have the preeminence in the nation since they were leaders of the tribe descended from the firstborn son of Jacob, who was Reuben.

The rebellion against religious authority and political authority affirmed that they, the members, were holy, and therefore Moses

167

and Aaron had no right to take supremacy over them. Moses summoned them all to appear before God the next day in order for God Himself to decide who was in the right. The next day, the earth opened her mouth and swallowed up all the men and their houses that rebelled against the appointed leaders God set in Moses and Aaron. But God showed mercy to the children of Korah and spared them even though Korah rebelled and was destroyed.

In 1 Chronicles 6, we see the lineage of Korah and find that the prophet Samuel, who later anointed both King David and Solomon, was a descendant of Korah. God projects Himself through time to fulfill His own purpose and plan. Wow! The Sons of Korah were temple singers and keepers of the sacred furniture. King David appointed them over all praise and worship. It is noted King David dedicated Psalm 42-49, to the Sons of Korah. These are some of the most beloved Psalms of all believers.

Let's look at the number 2,430 and the word "Cheylah" again. For you math nerds, the number 2,430 will factor 22 times. Remember there are 22 letters in the Hebrew Alphabet? Use 22 and divide it by God's number 7 for completeness, perfection, and unity. 22 divided by 7 is a good approximation of π (Pi – 3.14) – the ratio of a circle's circumference to its diameter. Used in the Geometric formula for solving the area of a circle $(A = \pi r^2)$. Pi times the Radius squared. Wouldn't your high school math teacher be proud of you now? A circle is the perfect shape of infinity without beginning or ending. The *Infinity Symbol* is written with a figure eight lying on its side (∞). How can this be? In Revelation 1:8 Jesus says, *"I am Alpha and Omega, the beginning and the ending, saith the Lord, which is, and which was, and which is to come, the Almighty."*

The number eight is like the mathematical symbol for infinity (∞) in a vertical position. Merriam-Webster's Dictionary defines the word infinity as: the quality of being infinite: unlimited extent of time, space, or quantity: boundlessness; an indefinitely great number or amount, an infinity of stars; the limit of the value of a function or variable when it tends to become numerically larger than any preassigned finite number; a part of a geometric magnitude that lies beyond any part whose distance from a given reference position is finite; a transfinite number, a distance so great that the rays of light from a point source at that distance may be regarded as parallel.

A figure eight can be a symbol of infinity and as shown previously, is the personal number of Jesus! Has God revealed Himself in mathematics? After having shown that the number of Jesus is 888, does the number eight signify anything else? Is the number eight related to Jesus and His resurrection? Jesus showed Himself alive eight times after His resurrection. His first appearance alive was to Mary Magdalene (Mark 16:9-11). He then showed Himself to two disciples traveling to Emmaus (Luke 24). Next, He appeared to all the disciples except Thomas (John 20:19-24) then a week later to all them when Thomas was present (John 20:26-29). According to the Apostle Paul, Jesus was seen by 500 believers at one time (1 Corinthians 15:4-7). Jesus also met his disciples at the appointed place in Galilee (Matthew 28:16-17) and on Galilee's shores (John 21:1-24). His final meeting was on the Mount of Olives, where He gave His followers instructions before ascending into heaven (Acts 1).

I suggest that the number eight has been chosen by God to emphasize the infiniteness of God, and the truth of the Trinity (Father, Son, and the Holy Spirit). God, the creator, made everything and ordained man to a special place of design and understanding. The associations of mathematics both within itself and to other truths are due to the sustenance of the Word of Jesus Christ.

Mathematics certainly adheres to Jesus Christ as I have pointed out. As we continue to dive deeper, we see more of the mysteries of Jesus revealed in mathematics. Using Gematria, the word Cheylah has a numerical value of 53. It is a prime number and will not factor. Jesus also reminds us He alone, *"... is the way, the truth, the life, and the only way to the father."*

John 14:6

The number 53 is composed of the digits 5 and 3 and is reduced to the single digit 8 (5 + 3 = 8). Thus the numerology number 53 principle is based on the essence of the number eight. There's that number of eight again, the sign of the new covenant (see Hebrews 8:8).

The term "I AM' is mentioned 53 times in the Gospel of Saint John. In the Book of Isaiah Chapter 53, verse 5 says, *"But he was wounded for our transgressions, he was bruised for our iniquities: the chastisement of our peace was upon him; and with his stripes, we are healed."* Isaiah Chapter 53 is the prophecy of the suffering servant (messiah) in detail sent to redeem Israel of its iniquities written in the Old Testament. This was fulfilled perfectly as written with the crucifixion of Jesus. Yeshua!

I found other related words with a numerical value of 53 in Gematria, the words; Stone, Prophecy, Message, Jubilee, and Torah. Are you kidding me? What can the Sons of Issachar discern from that word relationship?

Psalm 118:22, *"The **stone** which the builders refused is become the head stone of the corner."* The stone in this verse is Jesus Christ! Everything within this study points to God's divine redemption with Jesus Christ revealed from a single word study from the elevation of the Temple Mount! This is crazy! It just proves that the Word of God was divinely inspired and written. Isn't God's Word awesome to break down?

I must say, one of the greatest infringements of human and civil rights in the Western democratic world has not garnered much attention. With strong arguments being made for religious freedom around the world; why are the Jews stopped from praying at their holiest site? When will the Jews be treated equally by other nations and be allowed to pray on the Temple Mount?

The Temple Mount is the holiest site to the Jews, which regard it as the place where God's divine presence is manifested. Due to its extreme sanctity, many Jews will not walk on the Mount itself, in order to avoid unintentionally entering the area where the *Holy of Holies* once stood. According to Rabbinical law, some aspect of the divine presence is still present at the site. It was from the Holy of Holies that the High Priest communicated directly with God.

According to the rabbinic elders whose debates produced the Talmud (written oral traditions), it was from here the world expanded into its present form and where God gathered the dust used to create the first man, *Adam*. Since at least the first century, the site has been associated with the name *Mount Moriah*, the name given in the Bible to the location of *Abraham's Binding of Isaac* (Genesis 22) where he heard God's oath to bless all the nations. Both Jewish and Christian traditions immortalize this important place.

Jewish connection and reverence to the site arguably stems from the fact that it contains the *Foundation Stone,* which, according to the rabbis of the Talmud, was the spot where the world was created and expanded into its current form. It was afterward the site of the Holy of Holies of the Temple, the *Most Holy Place* in Judaism.

Jewish tradition names it as the location for a number of important events which occurred in the Bible, including the Binding of Isaac and *Jacob's dream* (Genesis 28:10-22). Similarly, the Bible also recounts that King David purchased a "threshing floor" owned by *Araunah* the Jebusite (2 Samuel 24:24). Tradition locates it as being on this Mount.

According to the Bible, David wanted to construct a sanctuary there, but this land was left to his son Solomon, who completed the task in 950 BC with the construction of the *First Temple*. Ever since the destruction of the *Second Temple*, the Jews have endeavored to return to the Temple Mount. In 1948, after the establishment of the State of Israel, there was great joy after 2,000 years. Yet this ecstasy was incomplete as most of Jerusalem was still under Jordanian rule.

In 1967, *Motta Gur*, the commander of the division, which entered the Old City, famously said with a voice full of excitement, "The Temple Mount is in our hands! The Temple Mount is in our hands!" However, ever since these few seconds of excitement, the Temple Mount has been far from being in Jewish hands.

Although the Temple Mount came under Israel's jurisdiction, Israel has been extremely sensitive to the Muslim population, who also claim the site as one of their holiest sites as well. There is a Mosque built on that very location. During its long history, Jerusalem has been destroyed at least twice, besieged 23 times, attacked 52 times, captured and recaptured 44 times. There is not a more disputed parcel of real estate than the Temple Mount in Jerusalem. More blood has been shed for control over the Temple Mount than anywhere else in the world.

Today the Temple Mount is controlled by Jordanian Islamic clerical authorities; the *Waqf*, a type of Muslim property trust, was left in charge of the Temple Mount following Jerusalem's reunification in 1967. The decision to leave the Temple Mount in the hands of the Waqf was made by Defense Minister Moshe Dayan. Today only Muslims are allowed to worship on the site. They have removed every sign of any ancient Jewish presence on the Mount. Rebuilding the Temple today would truly be a sign of redemption for all religions from Muslim tyranny.

The very thought that anyone even questions the fact that Israel is and has always been the home of the Jewish people for thousands of years is just mind-boggling to me. If you have a mind and can read, the Bible says Jerusalem is the capital of the Jews and the Temple Mount belongs to them!

Nonetheless, Jews are often barred from entering the Temple Mount area. Those who can enter are followed closely by Waqf

Police to ensure they do not engage in prayer. If someone dares to pray, they are immediately arrested and barred from reentering the mount. In most places around the world, such blatant discrimination would be condemned as anti-Semitic.

Jews are forbidden from praying at their holiest of sites, and people around the world find this acceptable. One must wonder why human right organizations are not lining up to join the fight in condemning the Waqf. The only possible justification is fear. The world is afraid of the Muslim reaction to Jewish prayer on the Temple Mount.

Since a temple has been such an important fixture in the history of the Jews, many have wondered what the Bible says about a *Third Temple*. While biblical scriptures are not always as obvious as we would like, there are scriptural indications of another temple.

Based on prophecies in the Book of Daniel about sacrifices coming to a close at the end of the *"age of man"* and of an end-time *"Abomination of Desolation,"* many believe the Jews will be allowed to build another temple in Jerusalem prior to the return of Jesus Christ. I believe it too.

Daniel 8:9-14 speaks of *"a little horn"* that will cause the daily sacrifices to cease. This little horn will be a type of an end-time world religious *false prophet* that will be aligned with a new world ruler. This ruler will be called the *antichrist*, or the beast.

Daniel 9:27 says the (the antichrist) shall make peace for seven years with many and in the midst (middle) he shall cause the sacrifice to cease.

Daniel 11:31 and 12:11 states again of *"the daily sacrifice"* being taken away. Both of these two passages in the Book of Daniel speak of sacrifices coming to a close, leading many scholars to conclude that a temple will indeed be built in connection with an altar upon which these sacrifices will be offered.

In addition to these passages in the Book of Daniel, Jesus also spoke of an end-time *"Abomination of Desolation"* that would stand in the *"holy place"* (Matthew 24:15-16 and Mark 13:14). Both Jesus and the Apostle Paul prophesied that the *"Abomination of Desolation"* would occur in a future Jewish Temple near the time of Jesus' Second Coming.

The Apostle Paul says in 2 Thessalonians 2:3-4, *"Let no man deceive you by any means: for that day shall not come, except there come a falling away first, and that man of sin be revealed, the son of perdition; Who opposeth and exalteth himself above all that is called God, or that is worshipped; so that he as God sitteth in the temple of God, shewing himself that he is God."*

While it is very possible that the Jews will build another temple before the return of Jesus Christ, there are already people dedicated to fulfilling this expectation. It is also possible that the Jews will begin offering sacrifices on an altar without building a temple, as was done prior to the construction of the *Second Temple* (Ezra 3:1-6).

When is the *Third Temple* going to be built? That's the question the Jews have been asking since the destruction of the *Second Temple* by the Romans in 70 AD. There is a group called "The Temple Mount Faithful" who every year attempt to bring the *Cornerstone of the Temple* up to the Mount in Jerusalem. Their Goal is to take back the Temple Mount and commence building the *Third Temple* in preparation for the Messiah.

Bible researchers believe the phrase "holy place" means there will indeed be another temple, while others believe this phrase could also simply refer to Jerusalem. Today the Temple Mount has at its center, the *Dome of the Rock*, an Islamic place of worship. However, is there another holy place? Is Mount Zion a possibility?

Zion is a place-name often used as an alternative expression for Jerusalem. It is also commonly referred to a specific mountain near Jerusalem (Mount Zion), on which stood a Jebusite fortress later named the *City of David*. The Bible records in 2 Samuel 5:7, David captured the *Jebusite* strong hold at Zion and later made Jerusalem the capital of Israel. David dwelt in the fort and called it the City of David.

Why did David choose Zion to pitch his tent (tabernacle)? Scriptures never really explain why David chose Jerusalem as his capital. However, he did have strong theological reasons for thinking it to be the best place as the capital for God's chosen people. This is where Abraham (then Abram) paid tithes (Hebrews 7:9-10) to *Melchizedek*, the King-Priest of the Most High God. The righteous king blessed Abram as the receiver of the covenant and then brought forth him bread and wine (see Genesis 14:17-20).

"And I will establish my covenant between me and thee and thy seed after thee in their generations for an everlasting covenant, to be a God unto thee, and to thy seed after thee."
Genesis 17:7

Who was *Melchizedek*? In the Hebraic Book of Jasher 16:11-12 (Joshua 10:13 and 2 Samuel 1:18 mentions this book) more is given about Melchizedek. *"And Adonizedek, King of Jerusalem, the same was Shem, the 'righteous son' of Noah, went out with his men to meet Abram and his people, with bread and wine and they remained together in the Valley of Melech. Abram gave him a tenth from all that he had brought from the spoil of his enemies, for Adonizedek was a king-priest before God."*

Melchizedek, David, and Jesus Christ are said to be in the forever priesthood of Melchizedek. David is named into the Melchizedek priesthood in Psalm 110:1-4, *"The Lord said unto my Lord, Sit thou at my right hand, until I make thine enemies thy footstool. The Lord shall send the rod of thy strength out of Zion: rule thou in the midst of thine enemies. Thy people shall be willing in the day of thy power, in the beauties of holiness from the womb of the morning: thou has the dew of thy youth. The Lord hath sworn, and will not repent; Thou art a priest for ever after the order of Melchizedek."*

Jesus Christ is the Highest King-Priest in the Melchizedek Priesthood in Hebrews 7:15-17, *"And it is yet far more evident: for that after the similitude of Melchizedek there ariseth another priest, who is made, not after the law of a carnal commandment, but after the power of an endless life. For he testifieth, Thou art a priest for ever after the order of Melchizedek."*

Why did Abram pay tithe to Melchizedek? In the beginning, man was created in the image of God. We were created to be God-like and Adam and Eve walked and talked with God in the *Garden of Eden.* The first thing recorded that God said to Adam was, *"And God blessed them, and God said unto them, be fruitful, and multiply, and replenish the earth, and subdue it: and have dominion over the fish of the sea, and over the fowl of the air, and over every living thing that moveth upon the earth."*

Genesis 1:28

Adam was the firstborn among men, and the firstborn calling is a king-priest calling or a "royal priesthood." In order to rule over the earth (have dominion over it), you must be a king and a priest. This is a pattern throughout all of scripture. The firstborn priesthood is necessary because any dominion over the earth is delegated and dispatched by He Who is Lord over all. Officiating on behalf of the Almighty to His subjects and in return, representing them to Him.

Adam was king-priest until he died. At the time of his death, the oldest firstborn living on the earth inherited the role of carrying on that kingly priesthood in the earth was *Seth.* The firstborn priesthood came through the godly line of Adam through Seth, and following down in time; it passed to Noah in the line of the priesthood. When Noah died, *Shem* inherited the firstborn blessing.

Shem died and handed the priesthood on to Abraham. For the timeline of the Genesis patriarchs, we can estimate it using the ages given in the Book of Genesis and the Book of Jubilees. Scholars start with the creation of Adam and add the information of the generations; when biblical scholars calculate, by adding these year's together, they prove that it was 1,948 years between Adam and Abraham. Can the Sons of Issachar discern anything from this? You'll get it in a minute!

But was Abraham a firstborn? The fact is that because he was a righteous man, the birthright was transferred to him, and he offered sacrifices. It says, *"...and offered him up for a burnt offering in the stead of his son."*

When Abraham died, he handed it on to Isaac. Isaac handed it on to Jacob. But was Jacob a firstborn? No; but you find that Jacob cunningly took it (the birthright) from Esau. He said to him in Genesis 25:31 *"Sell me first thy birthright."*

In time, Jacob had the function of the king-priest birthright blessing. Judah was blessed with the king-priest office. Joseph was given the birthright blessing (material blessing) through Ephraim and Manasseh. The *Levites* were given the priesthood following the incident of the golden calf through Aaron.

Therefore, all those are of Abraham come under the Melchizedek Priesthood. So, we see that this priesthood of the firstborn, the Melchizedek order of priesthood, passed on down from Adam down through their descendants to Noah, to Shem, and then to Abraham. From Abraham it was passed to Isaac, then Jacob, who became Israel.

Josephus, a Jewish historian who lived in the first century after Jesus Christ, knew of the tradition that Melchizedek was the first to officiate as king-priest of the Most High God and offered up burnt sacrifice in Zion. Where in Zion?

177

Zion is the place where David first brought the *Ark of the Covenant* to Jerusalem and introduced *Psalmist* worship with loud praise; all the house of Israel played musical instruments such as harps, timbrels, cornets, and cymbals when the Ark was placed *"inside the tent David had pitched for it"* (David's Tabernacle). The presence of God (the Ark) was open to all people -a picture of our access to God through Christ- in contrast to the *Tabernacle of Moses* where only the High Priest could enter once a year.

After placing the Ark in the tent, David established an order of worship that continued through his reign. Singers and musicians were employed to praise, giving thanks and prayer before the Ark of God. Twenty-four hour-a-day worship could be heard from Zion. David's Tabernacle was erected in a visible place on Mount Zion. All who entered the city could see the glory of God and hear the praises of God. Zion had become the worship capital of Israel. That was the reason God said, *"This is my resting place forever; here I will dwell, for I have desired it"*

Psalm 132:13-14

David was a true worshiper of God. He didn't just go through the rituals. His worship was unreserved from his heart. We read in Psalm 27:4, *"One thing I have desired of the LORD, that will I seek: that I may dwell in the house of the LORD all the days of my life, to behold the beauty of the LORD, and to inquire in His temple."*

In David's day, there was no temple; there was only the tent he had pitched. So when David talks about worship and his prayer, he's not talking so much about formal rituals and ceremonies, but rather something that came from deep within his heart. David speaks about prayer as a *"seeking after."* He speaks about worship in terms of *"beholding the beauty of the Lord."* For David, it was all about a personal relationship with God.

When David came to Jerusalem, he dressed as a king-priest (descendant of Judah), and those who were carrying the Ark of God had taken six steps, he sacrificed a bull and a fattened calf and offered up burnt sacrifice. He blessed the people and gave them bread and wine like Melchizedek had done before with Abraham. In doing so, David recognized God's covenant with Abraham and God recognized His covenant with the House of David. Through *thy seed* the throne of His kingdom forever will be established (see 2 Samuel 7:12-13).

David later gave instructions in I Kings 1:33-35, for his son Solomon to be anointed at the *Gihon Spring*. *"The king also said unto them, take with you the servants of your lord, and cause Solomon my son to ride upon mine own mule, and bring him down to Gihon. And let Zadok the priest and Nathan the prophet anoint him there king over Israel: and blow ye with the trumpet, and say, God save King Solomon. Then ye shall come up after him, that he may come and sit upon my throne; for he shall be king in my stead: and I have appointed him to be ruler over Israel and over Judah."*

The source of Jerusalem's only "life-giving water" is the Gihon Spring; which flows through *Hezekiah's Tunnel* into the *Pool of Siloam*, the place where Jesus healed the blind man (John 9:1-10) and also where the Jewish people would gather for the Feasts of the Lord. Three times a year, all men had to come to the *mikvah* (ritual bath) in the pool and from there ascend to Temple Mount. Hezekiah's Tunnel was cut in the bedrock 1,750 feet underneath the City of David in Jerusalem before 701 BC. This was during the reign of King Hezekiah of Judah. The tunnel is mentioned in 2 Kings 20:20 in the Bible.

God is revealing His promises; Bible prophesies are being fulfilled in Israel today. Isaiah 52:2 says, *"Shake thyself from the dust; arise, and sit down, O Jerusalem: loose thyself from the bands of thy neck, O captive daughter of Zion."*

Israel Antiquities Authority researchers have re-exposed a stretch of road in Jerusalem dating to the Second Temple period that is believed to have been used by pilgrims on their ascent to the Temple. The *Jerusalem Pilgrim Road* is an ancient road used by ritual processions ascending from the Pool of Siloam in the City of David at Zion to the Temple Mount via the *Hulda Gates* in the Southern Wall. During the temple period, on the last day of the Feast of Tabernacles; a priest would draw water from the Pool of Siloam with a golden vessel and descend up this road to the temple to pour "living water" upon the altar.

Also, recent excavations around the Gihon Spring have uncovered a massive 3,800 year-old fortress, called the "Spring Citadel" by archaeologists. According to *Oriya Dasberg*, director of development in the City of David, "The Spring Citadel was built in order to save and protect the water of the city from enemies coming to conquer it, as well as to protect the people going down to the spring to get water and bring it back up to the city."

About 1,000 feet south of the Temple Mount, the remains of an ancient temple have been discovered. This discovery is just a few feet from the Gihon Spring with a stone pillar near its entrance. Not known to many, the underground holy sanctuary just above and west of the spring has been recently found cut from bedrock at the Spring Citadel.

It is believed to be from the time of Melchizedek. Wrap your brain around that for a minute. Spring water was essential in the purification ceremony with the blood of the beasts that were killed; it was a requirement that they be purified with spring water and ointment. Spring water (moving pure water) and ointments (olive oil) were absolute essential needs for purification rituals. The only running and the only spring water available in Jerusalem was the Gihon Spring, which was in the City of David.

This is the only worship sanctuary ever found in the City of David. Inside the chamber, there are grooves cut into the bedrock for an olive press and sacrifice tables, and loops cut into the walls to secure animals. To the left of the olive press is a long channel, cut into the floor designed to drain off blood. The narrow groves, hand cut into the bedrock, wash away the blood with water from the spring; it is a gushing forth of a "fountain of blood" to wash our sins away (see Revelation 1:5).

This chamber could be the first dwelling place of the "holy divine presence of God," on earth, the *Shekinah* in Zion, where Melchizedek offered up sacrifice. We could think of this spot as "Temple Ground Zero."

What is the Shekinah glory? The word Shekinah does not appear in the Bible, but the concept clearly does. Jewish rabbis coined this extra-biblical expression, a form of a Hebrew word that literally means "he caused to dwell," signifying that it was a holy divine visitation of the presence of the Lord God on the earth.

The chamber is an ancient area of worship and praying where people connected with God. Could the chamber be the place of Genesis 14:17-20 were Abram paid tithes to Melchizedek? How about the house of God in Genesis 28:10-22?

Recall when Jacob feared for his life and fled from his brother Esau? He rested for a night and while sleeping dreamed of a staircase upon which angles were ascending and descending through an open window in heaven. He saw at the top of the staircase the Lord and was promised blessings onto his descendants and all families of the earth. When he awoke he determined he had been sleeping near the *"gate of heaven"* and the house of God. He took the stone which had been at his head and set it up as a pillar and anointed it with oil. The Bible states Jacob called this place *"Bethel,"* the house of God. He would have known of this shelter and a place of fresh running water from his grandfather Abraham and his father Isaac. I suggest the story in Genesis 28:10-22 is in the same place as the story in Genesis 14:17-20.

Is this also why David chose Zion for the place to set the "Ark of the Covenant" inside his tent (David's Tabernacle) to be near the house of God? The Bible reads in Psalm 46:4, *"There is a river whose streams make glad the city of God, the holy place where the Most High dwells."*

"In Salem also is His tabernacle, and His dwelling place in Zion."
Psalm 76:2

"The Lord loveth the gates of Zion more than all the dwellings of Jacob."
Psalm 87:2

"The LORD also shall roar out of Zion, and utter his voice from Jerusalem; and the heavens and the earth shall shake: but the LORD will be the hope of his people, and the strength of the children of Israel. So shall ye know that I am the LORD your God dwelling in Zion, my holy mountain: then shall Jerusalem be holy, and there shall no strangers pass through her anymore."
Joel 3:16-17

"And in mercy shall the throne be established: and he shall sit upon it in truth in the tabernacle of David, judging, and seeking judgment, and hasting righteousness."
Isaiah 16:5

"Thus saith the LORD; I am returned unto Zion, and will dwell in the midst of Jerusalem: and Jerusalem shall be called a city of truth; and the mountain of the LORD of hosts the holy mountain."
Zechariah 8:3

Is it possible that Melchizedek's recently unearthed underground chamber at the "Spring Citadel" could be a place of future "signs and wonders" for Israel? Future archeological discoveries may also be found nearby the citadel like the tomb of David and his successors. The tombs have never been found. Can you imagine what a historic event that would be? The Bible states clearly in (I Kings 2:10) that David was buried in the City of David, as well as his son Solomon (see 1 Kings 11:43).

God has promised to restore the "Tabernacle of David" and to establish the "mountain of the House of the Lord." He has promised to gather all nations and teach His paths before His return.

The Bible says in Amos 9:11-12, *"In that day I will raise up the tabernacle of David that is fallen, and close up the breaches thereof; and I will raise up his ruins, and I will build it as in the days of old. That they may possess the remnant of Edom, and of all the heathen, which are called by my name, saith the Lord that doeth this."*

The prophecy given by Amos, said the reason for the restoration of David's Tabernacle was that the remnant of Edom and the Gentiles called by His name would be possessed. Edom was the name given to *Esau* and his descendants. Esau was Isaac's son who sold his birthright to Jacob for a bowl of soup. God is interested in saving all those who have sold their birthright, which all of mankind did, through Adam, including the descendants of Esau. It is God's will that none should perish but that all (Jews and Gentiles) should come to repentance and have access to Him through Jesus Christ.

In the Book of Acts, Chapter 15, the apostles met for council in Jerusalem to discuss how to assimilate into the church the many Gentiles who had become believers. With much debate, the Apostle Peter related how the Holy Spirit fell at the house of *Cornelius*, a devoted man, but still a Gentile.

The Apostle James refers to scripture and stands to proclaim by inspiration of the Holy Spirit, that the event was in accordance with the prophecy of Amos 9:11-12. He then agrees with what was written and states the following:

"After this I will return, and will build again the tabernacle of David, which is fallen down; and I will build again the ruins

thereof, and I will set it up: That the residue of men might seek after the Lord, and all the Gentiles, upon whom my name is called, saith the Lord, who doeth all these things."

Acts 15:16-17

God has promised that the Tabernacle of David would be rebuilt as it was in the days of old. He started the rebuilding process at Pentecost with the Jews and continued it in the Gentile house of Cornelius. His Word is to bring us back to His path in the last days.

The pattern of the Tabernacle is now being manifested inside the hearts of believers and being known to the people of God. This is the true pattern of praise, worship, and intimacy with God that He has always intended for His people. God doesn't want to live in a building; He wants to live in your heart!

God's desire is to restore the same spirit of worship in the heart of believers that was characterized with David's Tabernacle. He not only desires to find His resting place in the worship of His people, but also that His people will worship and exalt Him in such a way that His name is known, His glory is manifested, and all men are drawn to Him. Sing a new song to the Lord! Let the whole earth sing to the Lord! Sing to the Lord; bless His name. Each day proclaim the good news that He saves (see Psalm 96:1-2).

Since David was a man after God's own heart, one may logically begin to ask, how do we get a heart like David and a relationship with God the way he did? David's life as a Psalmist and his relationship and interaction with the holy divine presence of God were introduced as the pattern for all subsequent generations of believers and worshipers to follow.

"I will praise thee, O Lord, with my whole heart; I will shew forth all thy marvelous works. I will be glad and rejoice in thee: I will sing praise to thy name, O thou most High."

Psalm 9:1-2

"Keep me as the apple of the eye, hide me under the shadow of thy wings."

Psalm 17:8

"I will love thee, O Lord, my strength."

Psalm 18:1

"The LORD is my light and my salvation; whom shall I fear? The LORD is the strength of my life; of whom shall I be afraid?"

Psalm 27:1

"He that dwelleth in the secret place of the most High shall abide under the shadow of the Almighty."

Psalm 91:1

The rebuilding of David's fallen tabernacle in the last days is a picture of a great end-time revival, the ***"Third Major Wave of Rain."*** It will expand the borders of God's kingdom among the nations, through evangelism. The restoration of David's Tabernacle has everything to do with being engaged as the extension of Jesus Christ's rule on the earth through the conversion of souls.

The eyes of Israel have been darkened, that they may not see; they have been cut off and set aside (the natural olive branches). Salvation has come to the Gentiles, grafted in as "wild branches" of the good olive tree. They partake of the root and fatness of the olive tree with riches of the world; because of this, they have provoked the Jews into jealousy.

The Apostle Paul warned the Gentiles that some of their branches will be broken off due to unbelief; *"For if God spared not the natural branches, take heed lest He also spare not thee"* - Romans 11:21. No one is exempt from the consequences of rejecting God's plan. God will bring severity (judgements) to cut them off, but goodness, if they continue in belief.

When God is finished with the Gentiles (referred to as "The Fullness of the Gentiles"), His focus will change and all will be saved grafting Israel into the covenant again. He will remove the blindness and reinstate Israel. Israel was set aside because of unbelief. The Gentiles have favor because of their belief. They should not be proud or haughty over this fact but realize that God is capable of setting the Gentiles aside. This is precisely what He will do. There is coming a revival that will spread globally into all nations; revival will graft *"them both"* into the good olive tree under the Messiah (see Romans 11:10-27.)

The rebuilding of the Tabernacle of David points to this Holy Spirit revival. Rebuilding the Tabernacle of David is not only related to evangelism and the expansion of the kingdom in these last days, but also to a revival that contained the kind of prayer and worship which existed when David's tabernacle stood at Zion. God is rebuilding that kind of tabernacle where multitudes from the nations (both Jew and Gentile) will have the ability to come under God's protection and salvation covenant.

"Thou shalt arise, and have mercy upon Zion: for the time to favour her, yea, the set time, is come."

Psalm 102:13

PSALM 118

I want to recommend reading a good book, <u>Hidden Prophecies in the Psalms</u> by J.R. Church (1990). In this book, the author points out that the Psalms, besides being recognized for their poetic beauty and supplication to the Lord in times of trouble, are also highly prophetic in nature. They are part of the astounding 1/3 of the Bible that makes up Bible prophecy.

It is the opinion of the author that the prophetic nature of the Psalms also corresponds with years having to do with end time events. He begins with 1948 (Psalm 48) when the Jewish people re-established the State of Israel in fulfillment of God's promise to bring them back to the land of their birthright.

Interestingly, the placement of the Book of Psalms itself, in the order it appears in scripture, testifies to the significance of this date. Psalms is the 19th book from Genesis and the 48th book counting back from Revelation. You'll get it in a minute!

This is important because the events of 1948, with the re-establishment of Israel, began the count down for God's appointed *set time*. In Matthew 24:32-34, Jesus makes reference to this when he says, *"Now learn a parable of the fig tree; When his branch is yet tender, and putteth forth leaves, ye know that summer is nigh. So likewise ye, when ye shall see all these things, know that it is near, even at the doors. Verily I say to you, this generation shall not pass, till all these things be fulfilled."*

A biblical generation is known to be 70 years. When added to 1948, it will bring us to the 70th anniversary of the nation of Israel in 2018. If the Psalms are indeed prophetic as J.R. Church theorized, then what can we learn from examining Psalm 118? Will it correspond to our "times and seasons" for 2018?

Bible facts and trivia folks, this one is for you. How many chapters are there in the Bible? What is the center chapter in the Bible? What is the center verse in the Bible? Do you know? Let me help you. There are 1,189 chapters in the Bible. The center chapter is Psalm 118. There are 594 chapters before it and 594 chapters after it. The center verse in the Bible is Psalm 118:8, *"It is better to trust in the Lord than to put confidence in man."* Wow! Bullseye!

Here are some more trivia questions. What is the shortest chapter in the Bible? What is the longest chapter in the Bible? Can you figure it out by now? The shortest chapter in the Bible is Psalm 117, and the longest chapter in the Bible is Psalm 119. Psalm 118 is sandwiched between them! Why did God intentionally bring attention to this chapter? Do the Sons of Issachar discern anything yet?

When I personally began to analyze Psalm 118 for myself with a prophetic mindset, it practically spoke to me. I believe Psalm 118 may show us one of the greatest restoration events (Jubilee) in the future revealed for Israel. Let's examine an extraordinary event in Psalm 118:22-23 that took place during the cutting of the stones for the *First Temple. "The stone which the builders refused is become the head stone of the corner. This is the LORD's doing; it is marvelous in our eyes."*

Jesus also quoted this verse in reference to himself in Matthew 21:42 - Jesus said to them, *"Have you never read in the Scriptures, the stone which the builders rejected, the same is become the head of the corner: this is the LORD's doing, and it is marvelous in our eyes?"*

The stone is reference to the "Messiah," and the builders are the Jews. The Jews forced the crucifixion of Jesus Christ. The rejection by His own people was the Lord's doing, it was planned before the foundation of the world. Not only does Psalm 118 declare the coming of the Messiah, but it also predicts that the Messiah will be rejected. Jesus is many times referred to in the Bible as "The Stone" or "The Rock."

In ancient stone/masonry building, the cornerstone was the joining of two walls, tying them together. It was the visible corner of the foundation of a building and the starting point for all future building on that foundation. This single stone was the most costly because of its beauty and strength. It was also the largest, the most solid and carefully constructed stone. Casting aside the cornerstone would remove the possibility of any future building on that foundation. The cornerstone was the place where the building was joined together and the place where it rested.

The prophecy of the Messiah in Psalm 118 predicted that the leaders of Israel would believe that Jesus's claim to be the Messiah was a mistake. They would reject Him and cast Him aside, only to discover later, when He returns to earth the second time, that they had rejected their Chief Cornerstone. *"And one shall say unto him, What are these wounds in thine hands? Then he shall answer, Those with which I was wounded in the house of my friends."*

Zechariah 13:6

The Apostle Peter calls Jesus Christ the "living stone," in I Peter 2:4-8, *"To whom coming, as unto a living stone, disallowed indeed of men, but chosen of God, and precious, ye also, as lively stones, are built up a spiritual house, a holy priesthood, to offer up spiritual sacrifices, acceptable to God by Jesus Christ. Wherefore also it is contained in the scriptures, behold, I lay in Zion a Chief Cornerstone, elect, precious: and he that believeth on Him shall not be confounded. Unto you therefore which believe He is precious: but unto them which is disobedient, the stone which the builders disallowed, the same is made the head of the corner."* And a stone of stumbling, and a rock of offense, even to them which stumble at the word, being disobedient: whereunto also they were appointed."*

What can we take away prophetically from Psalm 118? What is implied for the year 2018 for Israel and the United States with the 70th anniversary of the nation of Israel? Will 2018 bring a

Cornerstone to the Mount? Questions for the Sons of Issachar to discern!

The 70th anniversary will indeed be very prophetic; hold on to your seats my friends! Daniel the prophet spoke of 70 sevens that must be fulfilled in order for redemption to come. Jeremiah the prophet spoke of 70 years of judgment in which Israel would be enslaved to Babylon. The *First Temple* was destroyed in 586 BC and the *Second Temple* completed in 516 BC making it 70 years of redemption. The enslavement in Babylon, by the way, occurred because Israel did not keep the statutes of the Jubilee (Leviticus 25). In the year 2018, it will be 1,948 years since the destruction of the Second Temple in 70 AD.

Ecclesiastes 1:9 - *"The thing that hath been, it is that which shall be; and that which is done is that which shall be done: and there is no new thing under the sun."*

Christians need to pay careful attention to the development of what happens next. The events unfolding in Israel and the United States may be culminating with further "clashing of swords", with a war between the *Sons of Light and the Sons of Darkness*. The fate of the Temple Mount is an extreme emotional issue at the heart of the Israeli-Palestinian conflict for sure. Even the smallest change to very delicate arrangements pertaining to the site sparks tensions.

There could be a break out of war very soon in Israel with earth-shaking implications. However, the Bible is clear to those that come against Israel and God's will. *"And I will shake all nations and the desires of all nations shall come: and I will fill this house with glory, saith the Lord of hosts. The silver is mine, and the gold is mine, saith the Lord of hosts. The glory of this latter house shall be greater than of the former, saith the Lord of hosts: and in the place will I give peace, saith the Lord of hosts."*

Haggai 2:7-9

If war breaks out, Trump will stand with Israel like in the days of Cyrus. He will assist them in rebuilding any infrastructure and preserve the peace. In doing so, there is only one way to do this; decree to raise the Temple up!

I suggest the patterns of God show that the *Cornerstone* could be set for the future building of the *Third Temple,* soon. I believe Donald Trump will be instrumental in setting of that very *Cornerstone* of the temple in Jerusalem. Many in the world will declare Trump is evil for doing this.

"And it shall come to pass in the last days, that the mountain of the LORD'S house shall be established in the top of the mountains, and shall be exalted above the hills; and all nations shall flow unto it."

Isaiah 2:2

Despite all the controversies, the temple is already being prepared. In the article "Temple in Waiting" reported by Christian World News, Chaim Richman, director at the *Temple Institute* in Jerusalem says the temple is already underway. "The Temple Institute is actively engaged in the research and preparation of the resumption of service in the holy temple to the extent of actually preparing operational blueprints for the construction of the temple according to the most modern standards," he said.

The menorah is just one of several vessels being created for the next temple. It's covered with 95 pounds of pure gold and has a price tag of $2 million. Piece by piece, the *Third Temple* is taking shape, with priest's garments, vessels of copper, gold, and silver, and a new generation of Levite priests being specially trained for temple service.

"We have enough in place now to resume divine service and to build the temple," Richman said, "but obviously, a lot of things have to happen in order for this to happen." The article further states that Gershon Solomon leads a group called "The Temple

Mount Faithful." The group commissioned cornerstones for the *Third Temple*. The six-ton stones were consecrated with water from the biblical *Pool of Siloam* and were cut with diamonds.

Reconstruction of the *Third Temple* would be a critically important sign for those who follow Bible prophecy. Once these events start to occur there will be no denying that we are indeed living in the *End of Days*. But most people will view them as a natural progression of current affairs in today's society since some of these prophecies will take years to conclude.

Whether an individual understands prophecy or not, nothing will compare to one particular prophecy, the building of the *Third Temple* on the Temple Mount in Jerusalem. Some deny that a Jewish temple ever stood on the Temple Mount, but the Bible and history easily prove that wrong.

Throughout time, two Jewish temples have stood atop the Temple Mount in Jerusalem. With the fulfillment of many of the end time prophecies converging at the same time, and with current efforts calling for the building of the *Third Temple*, it is very likely that we will see construction begin before too long.

"And when these things begin to come to pass, then look up, and lift up your heads; for your redemption draweth nigh."
Luke 21:28

JUBILEE AMERICA'S SET TIME CONCLUSION

America is standing once again on the tipping point, right in the center of another perfect prophetic storm. What will America's Christians do? Will history record that this was our finest hour to stand up against tyranny? I am convinced that God is not finished with America. I suggest when all hope seems lost, that is when God parts the waters! I think this could be a Red Sea moment for the church in America with Jubilee. It is the *set time* for America!

It is a very exciting time to be alive; not since the time of Jesus has more prophecy has been fulfilled or is currently being fulfilled. Prophecy being fulfilled shows no doubt there is a God and His Word is sovereign!

What is America's unfinished assignment in the World? The United States has been the world's dominant economic and strong military force. We have been so uniquely blessed to bring stability to the world so that the Gospel can advance and nations can actually be brought into the kingdom of God. But we still have a lot of work to do! The current status of our economy is stagnant, but the Jubilee cycle shows better times are ahead for God's people and He is preparing Judah, Issachar, and Zebulun for revival! ***"The elect are going to see great provision for seven years to fulfill my harvest."***

"And the LORD shall make thee the head, and not the tail; and thou shalt be above only, and thou shalt not be beneath; if that thou hearken unto the commandments of the LORD thy God, which I command thee this day, to observe and to do them."
Deuteronomy 28:13

Every time you pick up the Bible, you are opening a book of freedom and liberty. Jesus is the true picture of Jubilee, the greatest picture of God's freedom and grace through Christ. Those in prison are those who are under a crushing debt of sin they could never repay. Jesus is the new king-priest setting prisoners free of debt that they owe because of their sin. Through Jesus' work on

193

the cross, those who become a part of His Kingdom receive liberty and forgiveness of all debt that they could never pay for themselves.

The Book of Acts church is stirring! Will you be a part of it? God is indeed rebuilding David's Tabernacle and waking up the slumbering saints with revival! He will send them into mobilization at a level not yet seen in our lifetime with the *"Third Major Wave of Rain!"* The Holy Spirit is headed our way! May I remind you of the Lord's words that were spoken to my spirit, *"There's fire on the mountain! It's raining in the high places!"*

More than ever, our responsibility at this *"set time"* in America is to subscribe ever more vigorously to the Great Commission (Matthew 28:18-20). There is coming soon opportunities through unfortunate events for outreach to preach the true gospel of Jesus Christ and save many souls for the kingdom. Will you do your part?

Prophetic clouds are again forming for yet another storm. Something is on the horizon, approaching at high speed, and there is nothing anyone can do to stop it! We must pray ourselves trough the next eyewall of the prophetic storm to reach the spiritual revival. Are you prepared to see more of God's Word revealed?

"The fear of the Lord is the beginning of wisdom."
Psalm 111:10

Many celestial signs in the heavens will be seen over a 12-month period along with major historical anniversaries. The number 12 can be found in 187 places in God's Word. Revelation alone has 22 occurrences of the number. The meaning of 12, which is considered a perfect number, is that it symbolizes God's power and authority, as well as serving as a perfect governmental foundation. It can also symbolize completeness for the nation of

194

Israel. Listed below are some interesting events over the next 12-month span in 2017-18, from Pentecost to Pentecost:

May 13, 2017 – **100th** Anniversaries of the Apparitions of Fatima.
May 31, 2017 - Festival of Weeks "Pentecost".
June 7, 2017 – **50th** Anniversary of Jerusalem Unified.
June 17, 2017 – 45th Anniversary of the Watergate Break-in.
August 1, 2017 – 9th of Av, commemorating the destruction of the two Temples.
August 21, 2017 – The Great American Solar Eclipse across the United States.
August 21, 2017 – 1st Day of Elul, beginning of Teshuva.
August 21, 2017 – 40 Days before the Day of Atonement.
September 21-23, 2017 – Feast of Trumpets.
September 23, 2017 - The Sign of the Zodiac of Revelation 12.
September 23, 2017 – Fall Equinox.
September 30, 2017 – Day of Atonement.
October 5, 2017 – Feast of Tabernacles.
October 12, 2017 – Asteroid 2012 TC4 will pass 4,200 miles from earth.
October 12, 2017 – **525th** Anniversary of Columbus's discovery of America.
October 13, 2017 – **100th** Anniversary of the Miracle of the Sun at Fatima.
October 25, 2017- **100th** Anniversary of Red October, the Bolshevik Revolution in Russia.
October 31, 2017 – **500th** Anniversary of the Protestant Reformation.
November 2, 2017 – **100th** Anniversary of the Balfour Declaration.
December 11, 2017 – **100th** Anniversary of General Edmund Allenby leading the British Egyptian Expeditionary Force into Jerusalem through the Jaffa Gate.
December 12, 2017 – Jewish festival of rededication "Hanukkah" the Festival of Lights.
February 9-25, 2018 - The Winter Olympics are to be held in Pyeongchang, South Korea.

March 20, 2018 - Spring Equinox.
March 31, 2018 – Passover.
April 1, 2018 – Feast of Unleavened Bread.
April 6, 2018 – Feast of First Fruits.
May 14, 2018 – **70th** Anniversary of the State of Israel.
May 20, 2018 – Festival of Weeks "Pentecost".

Jesus said in Matthew 24:6-13, *"And ye shall hear of wars and rumors of wars: see that ye be not troubled: for all these things must come to pass, but the end is not yet. For nation shall rise against nation, and kingdom against kingdom: and there shall be famines, and pestilences, and earthquakes, in divers places. All these are the beginning of sorrows. Then shall they deliver you up to be afflicted, and shall kill you: and ye shall be hated of all nations for my name's sake. And then shall many be offended, and shall betray one another, and shall hate one another. And many false prophets shall rise, and shall deceive many. And because iniquity shall abound, the love of many shall wax cold. But he that shall endure unto the end, the same shall be saved."*

Has God been trying to get our attention? Are you right in your heart? Are you still walking in darkness? It's not what you know; it's who you know! Jesus will carry you through every storm in your life and give you strength to press through it. Accepting Jesus as your savior is truly the better way, the only way to live! I invite you today to walk in the light and accept Yeshua! Jesus said, *"Keep company with me and you'll learn to live freely and lightly."*

"Revival"
Karen Peck and New River

Folks are coming from far and wide
Old camp meeting on the county line
101 yeah and it feels like revival
Red back hymnals folding chair canvas tent in open air
Saw dust floor and a Holy Ghost prayer revival

Preachers preaching all day long
Sing another stanza of that hallelujah song
We're gonna shout the glory down
Join in that heavenly sound toe tapping hand clapping revival
We're gonna stand and testify, hands lifted up to the sky
Faith stirring shakes the earth revival

Let's head on down to the river side muddy water with robes of white
One more sinner gonna be baptized
All things have passed away, go down a sinner come up saint
We're gonna shout the glory down
Join in that heavenly sound, toe tapping hand clapping revival
We're gonna stand and testify, hands lifted up to the sky
Faith stirring shakes the earth revival
Time moves on and it's not the same my name has changed
and my face is not the same but there is one thing that remains the same
revival

AUTHOR BIO

Richard McCasland is a blood-member of the Oklahoma Choctaw Tribe. He was raised in a traditional Christian farm-family in Southeastern Oklahoma. In his youth, he held a paper route, worked as a paperboy, and enjoyed playing baseball. He was an active member in the international evangelical Christian organization Awana Club and both the 4-H Clubs and the Future Farmers of America. Attending college, he was elected class president twice by his peers and was a member of a National Champion Junior College Livestock Judging Team.

While in college, he was employed during the summers with the Southwestern Company in Nashville, Tennessee as a student sales manager for a door-to-door sales team in Alabama and Kentucky. He completed his education at Oklahoma State University and graduated with degrees in both Agricultural Economics and Accounting. He has worked as a financial accounting consultant for a large regional accounting firm. He has also been a Chief Financial Officer of a west coast construction company specializing in soil and water remediation. He was responsible for business development and worked closely with other minority owned SBA 8(a) Firms and customers. Some of those included the Army Corp of Engineers, Northrop Grumman Marine Systems, Union Pacific Railroad, and the US Navy.

Rich is a fervent student of Bible Prophecy, the Word of God, frequent traveler to and supporter of the nation of Israel. For more than two decades, he has been a Registered Financial Advisor in Oklahoma City. He currently resides in Stillwater, Oklahoma as a father of three beautiful children, two grandchildren, and owner of McCasland Farms, a small purebred Berkshire Swine Farm.

CPSIA information can be obtained
at www.ICGtesting.com
Printed in the USA
LVHW032248291018
595217LV00014B/756/P